JEWISH HOLIDAYS

By the Same Author

JEWISH HOLIDAYS

Facts, Activities, and Crafts

SUSAN GOLD PURDY

J. B. LIPPINCOTT COMPANY
Philadelphia   *New York*

To my grandmother
CLARA JOSLIN
and to the memory of my grandparents
HARRY JOSLIN
and
REBECCA AND JACOB GOLD

ACKNOWLEDGMENTS

For information and invaluable assistance in the research and preparation of this book, the author wishes to express her indebtedness and gratitude to all who helped, including Dr. Shlomo Noble, Secretary, Commission on Research, YIVO Institute for Jewish Research; Miss Dina Abramowicz, Librarian, YIVO; Rabbi Samuel Schwartz; Israel Government Tourist Office; Israel Information Service; Jewish National Fund; my parents Harold and Frances Gold; Nancy Gold; Mrs. Beatrice Joslin; and my husband, Geoffrey Purdy. The author accepts full responsibility for the material.

TABLE OF CONTENTS

INTRODUCTION

The Jewish religion is a rich and colorful tapestry woven of laws, history, folklore, culture, and tradition. The highlights in this tapestry are the holidays, which come with welcome regularity to brighten the year. The traditional prayers, rituals, foods, legends, songs, dances, and other activities that are part of each holiday unite Jews throughout the world and remind them of the meaning of Judaism.

There are several different types of Jewish holidays. The most important are the High Holy Days of *Rosh Hashanah* (New Year) and *Yom Kippur* (Day of Atonement). The two festivals related to the moon are *Shabbat* (Sabbath) and *Rosh Hodesh* (Beginning of a New Moon). Originally agricultural festivals, *Pesach* (Passover), *Shavuot* (Festival of Weeks), and *Succot* (Feast of the Ingathering or Booths) came to be known as the pilgrimage festivals, or *Regalim,* (from the Hebrew word *regal,* meaning "foot"). In biblical times, Jews celebrated these festivals by making pilgrimages and bringing harvest offerings to the Temple. The minor festivals and commemorative days are *Hanukah* (Feast of Dedication), *Tu Bishvat* (New Year of the Trees), *Purim* (Festival of Lots), *Lag B'Omer* (Thirty-third Day of the Omer), *Yom Ha'azmaut* (Israeli Independence Day), and *Tisha B'Av* (Ninth Day of Av).

It is hoped that this book will contribute to a basic understanding of the Jewish holidays while at the same time adding some fresh ideas to the traditional holiday activities. Only a few recipes have been included (others may be found in Jewish cookbooks in a library), as the emphasis is primarily upon craft activities. There is wide variety among the projects included. Some are easy and quick to make, others take a little more time and patience. At the end of this book, you will find a list of all the materials used in the projects, and directions for tracing and transferring patterns and scoring paper. Before beginning any project, read all the directions through to the end. Use the suggestions in this book as a starting place for making up your own imaginative designs and decorations. Combine unusual materials, experiment, have fun, and you will create beautiful and joyful holidays.

NOTES ON
SPELLING AND PRONUNCIATION

The Hebrew language uses a different alphabet than English, and thus has several different sounds. When Hebrew words are translated into the sounds and alphabet of English, the spellings vary widely. You will find, for example, the spellings Sukkoth, Sukkot, Succot, Succoth, and Succos, or Chanukah, Hanukah, and Hanukkah. This variation depends first upon whether the pronunciation in Hebrew is Ashkenazic or Sephardic (*see below*), and second, upon the translator himself, who chooses the English spelling he feels most closely resembles the Hebrew sound.

Jews living in Germany and most of northern and eastern Europe are known as *Ashkenazim*, while the Jews of Spanish and Portuguese origin are known as *Sephardim*. They differ in rituals and customs as well as in their pronunciation of Hebrew. The Ashkenazim spoke German, and developed the *Yiddish* language, while the Sephardim spoke Spanish and their own dialect known as *Ladino*. The Sephardic pronunciation of Hebrew has been adopted in Israel and in Mediterranean Jewish communities, and is becoming increasingly popular for modern spoken Hebrew, though the Ashkenazic pronunciation is still often used in the United States.

The difference between the two is shown for example, by words ending in the Hebrew sound *th* or *t;* the Ashkenazic pronunciation of this sound is *s*, while the Sephardic pronunciation is *t*. Throughout this book, we have used the Sephardic spelling for the Hebrew words transliterated into English. Sephardic pronunciation then is as follows:

a—pronounced as in car
e—as in ten
ee—as in three
i—as in slim
o—as in hope
u—as in tube
h—as in hat, or guttural *kh sound* made in back of throat
ch, kh—as in the Scottish *loch*, guttural *kh* sound made in back of throat

THE HEBREW CALENDAR

Since men first lived on the earth, they have marked the passage of time. They awoke and worked when the sun rose, they slept when night's darkness fell. They notched sticks and knotted ropes to keep track as they counted their ages by the number of summers or winters they had seen. They noticed changes in the seasons and they watched the changing positions of the sun and moon. When men began formally to record time's passing by developing a calendar, they used the sun and the moon for guides.

The calendar that governs civil (nonreligious) life in the Western World is based upon a system that follows the movement of the earth around the sun. The complete solar (sun) year takes three hundred and sixty-five days plus five hours, forty-eight minutes and forty-six seconds. This extra quarter-day is collected for four years, until it makes one whole day, then added on at the end of February, making a leap year.

The Hebrew calendar is based upon the movement of the moon around the earth. It is a lunar calendar, and the Hebrew word for month, *yerah*, is derived from the word *yareah*, "moon" in Hebrew.

As the moon takes approximately twenty-nine and one half days to travel around the earth, the lunar year is made of twelve months of twenty-nine to thirty days each, making a year of three hundred and fifty-four days. To make the length of the lunar year equal that of the solar year, so that the holidays fall in their proper seasons, extra days must be added. Like the civil calendar, the Hebrew calendar also has a leap year. Seven times in each nineteen-year cycle (in the third, sixth, eighth, eleventh, fourteenth, seventeenth, and nineteenth years) a thirteenth month is added in the early spring, after the month of Adar. It is called *Adar Sheni* or *Bet Adar* (Second Adar).

About 1300 B.C.E.,* *Moses* introduced the first time system based upon a seven-day week. The number seven was used because each phase of the moon lasted approximately seven days. Moses adapted the system he had known as a child living in Egypt, but he built his calendar around weeks, in which the seventh day was kept as a holy day, or Sabbath. In the fourth century, the patriarch and scholar Hillel II fixed and made public the rules governing the Hebrew calendar. Before this time, the Jews depended solely upon their leaders to inform them, on *Rosh Hodesh*, about their holidays.

---

* Throughout this book we have followed the accepted procedure of using the terms B.C.E. (Before the Common Era) and C.E. (Common Era) corresponding to the Gregorian calendar's B.C. (Before Christ) and A.D. (*Anno Domini*). Therefore, a date such as 70 B.C.E. is the same as 70 B.C. and 1492 C.E. is the same as A.D. 1492.

ROSH HODESH

The appearance of each new moon is naturally the most important day in a lunar calendar, for it tells you when to begin each month. This day, called in Hebrew *Rosh Hodesh,* literally "the beginning of a new moon," was in biblical times a most important holiday. On this day, the *Sanhedrin,* or High Court of Jerusalem, sounded the *shofar* (ram's horn) and proclaimed the official start of the new moon. News traveled slowly in those days, and it often took two days to reach Jews living outside Palestine. In order for all to have time to observe the new moon, the holiday was extended for two days. This custom carried over to other festivals, and today in most countries, though not in Israel, Orthodox and Conservative Jews continue the practice of celebrating holidays for at least two days. Reform Jews celebrate most holidays for the first day only. According to the Hebrew calendar, the day begins and ends with the sunset.

Though of less importance today, Rosh Hodesh is still observed as a holiday. Special prayers are said for peace and prosperity. In the synagogue, the rabbi announces the day on which the new moon and the new month will begin.

The Hebrew calendar, one of the oldest still in use in the world, is based upon the date 3761 B.C.E., traditionally believed by Jewish scholars to be the year in which the world was created. Therefore, the Hebrew calendar year 5729–5730 is equal to the year 1969 in the civil calendar. This civil system, also known as the Gregorian calendar, took the names of its months from the early Romans, while the Hebrew calendar borrowed many of its names from the ancient Babylonians, who also used a lunar cycle. Today, Jews use the lunar calendar to govern their religious life, and the solar, Gregorian calendar for their nonreligious life. The diagram following will show you how both systems fit together and where the holidays are located.

GREGORIAN CIVIL CALENDAR	HEBREW CALENDAR AND HOLIDAYS	
SEPTEMBER	TISHRI	ROSH HASHANAH YOM KIPPUR SUCCOT HOSHANAH RABBAH SHEMINI AZERET SIMHAT TORAH
OCTOBER	HESHVAN	
NOVEMBER	KISLEV	HANUKAH
DECEMBER	TEVET	
JANUARY	SHEVAT	TU BISHVAT
FEBRUARY	ADAR	PURIM
MARCH	NISAN	PESACH
APRIL	IYAR	YOM HA'AZMAUT LAG B'OMER
MAY	SIVAN	SHAVUOT
JUNE	TAMMUZ	
JULY	AV	TISHA B'AV
AUGUST	ELUL	

SHABBAT
(Sabbath)

In ancient times, before the liberation from Egypt (*see* Pesach, *page 60*), the Sabbath as we know it was not generally observed. At that time, its celebration was related to the moon, which was greatly revered. The moon has four phases during its month of about twenty-eight days, and it was believed to stand still briefly at the end of each period of approximately seven days. During the time that the moon "rested," men were forbidden to work. This day of rest carried over when, in later times, the Jewish religion became formalized. The Sabbath day was fixed and no longer depended upon the position of the moon.

The Bible tells us that God created the world in six days and on the seventh, the Sabbath, he rested. For men, too, the Sabbath is a day of rest and reflection. It is observed by Jews each week of the year from sundown on the sixth day, Friday, to sundown on the seventh day, Saturday. The Sabbath is the only holiday mentioned in the Ten Commandments ("Remember the Sabbath Day, to keep it holy"). Thus, it is one of the most important of all holidays and is welcomed with joy as the "Queen" or "Bride."

Today on the Sabbath, Orthodox Jews will neither work, ride, nor kindle any lights. Conservative and Reform Jews are more liberal in their observances of the Sabbath, but always this is a time for special preparations in the home. For this is a family holiday. Mother cleans the house and prepares the table with the finest linens, china, and silver. On the table she arranges the candles, which symbolize the light and joy brought by the Sabbath. There are always at least two candles, but in some homes there are additional candlesticks, one for each member of the family. Beside the candles, Mother places the ceremonial wine cup and the traditional two loaves of *challah*, braided white bread. Two loaves are used to recall the double portion of *manna* gathered by the wandering Jews on Friday to last them throughout the Sabbath. A white powderlike food substance, manna is believed to have miraculously fallen from heaven during the forty years of wandering.

Just before sundown Friday, Mother lights the Sabbath candles and recites a blessing over them. Then the family gathers for the Sabbath meal. Father says a special prayer for the Sabbath, recites the *Kiddush*, a traditional prayer sanctifying the wine, and blesses the bread. He then blesses the children and the meal begins. Often the meal includes *gefilte fish* (a combination of fresh-water fish chopped, shaped into balls, and cooked in fish stock, usually served cold), chicken soup and/or roast chicken, and a pudding or *kugel,* served in a round bowl to symbolize the whole round week. The Sabbath meal, which is especially blessed if shared with friends, may end with the singing of Sabbath songs.

At the close of the Sabbath, the *Havdalah* ceremony is observed. Havdalah comes from the Hebrew root *havdal,* meaning "separation," and the special prayers said during this ceremony honor the one day set apart from all others, and mark its end. An important part of the ceremony is the lighting of the multicolored, braided Havdalah candle. There are various interpretations of the candle. Some say it is in memory of Adam, the first man, who discovered fire. Others say it symbolizes the divine light in man and in the divine law, or that the braid represents the Sabbath interwoven with the weekdays. The aroma of fragrant spices fills the room during the Havdalah ceremony both to remind one of the sweetness of the Sabbath and to revive one's spirits after the sadness of parting with the "Sabbath Queen."

 ## SABBATH CANDLESTICK

For your Sabbath table, you can use just one of these candlesticks, for it holds two candles. Or, make additional candlesticks for each member of your family.

Materials: Self-hardening clay (about ¾ pound, does not require an armature), standard-size candles (about ¾″ diameter), ruler, orange stick or clay-modeling tool, can of water, emery board or sandpaper, newspapers, felt, fork, or other objects with interesting textures.

1. Read directions on package of self-hardening clay. *Read step 1, page 32.*

2. Cover work surface with newspapers. Model a roll of clay about 10″ long and 1″ thick. Curl ends of roll around, forming "S" as shown. Smooth over any cracks along curves.

(16)

3. Shape may be left in long "S" (*step 2*) or shortened by gently pressing curved ends toward center to compress shape. Make each end round. Smooth all sides and joints firmly with finger or modeling tool. Turn piece over and smooth sides of joints and entire bottom surface.

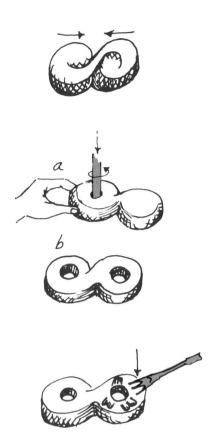

4. Turn piece right side up. Dip base of candle in water. Holding end of clay piece as shown, twist wet candle base into the center of each curl of the "S" (a). Make hole about ¾″ deep. Twist and lift candle to remove. Repeat at opposite end (b).

5. To give the candlestick a decorative patterned surface, press objects with interesting textures into surface of clay. For example, you might make dots with a pencil point or lines with fork tines (as shown). After making such decorations, replace candle, twist to reshape holes, then remove.

6. Set candlestick in warm place to dry. Clay is dry if it clicks when tapped gently and is a light color. Smooth dry clay with sandpaper or emery board. Paint candlestick with tempera paint (or spray with enamel paint). *Note:* If using more than one color, allow first coat to dry before adding second. When paint is dry, shellac or coat with clear krylon spray for glossy, durable finish.

7. Cut out a piece of felt and glue over bottom of candlestick to protect table top.

ROSH HASHANAH

The Jewish New Year is called *Rosh Hashanah*, or "Head of the Year." It is celebrated on the first two days of the month of Tishri (September–October), and begins the High Holy Days, the most sacred period of the year during which Jews devote themselves to prayer and self-judgment.

The first day of Tishri is also special for another reason: Jewish legend tells that on this day the world was created, and in honor of this event, children in some religious schools sing "Happy Birthday, World."

During the two days of Rosh Hashanah, Jews generally do no work, but remain in the synagogue to pray for the major part of the day. For this is the beginning of the Ten Days of Penitence during which God judges the lives of men and writes his judgment in the Book of Life. If one has lived a good life, one's fate may be written on Rosh Hashanah, but if not, one is given the next ten days in which to concentrate on begging forgiveness from whomever one may have wronged. Promises are made to live a better life in the coming year. Thus, this festival is also called *Yom Hazikaron*, "The Day of Remembrance," and *Yom Hadin*, "Day of Judgment."

Rosh Hashanah has still another name, *Yom Teruah*, "The Day of the Blowing of the Ram's Horn." The horn, in Hebrew *shofar*, is known as the symbol of God's calling his people together for self-improvement and self-judgment. The shofar has been used since ancient times, when the festival was known as the "Feast of the Trumpets." In the synagogue, the shofar is blown during the morning service on the first two days of Rosh Hashanah. During Elul, the month before Tishri, the shofar is sounded every morning to remind the congregation that Rosh Hashanah is approaching and they should begin to examine their consciences. According to the biblical story, the ram's horn is used because when Abraham was willing to sacrifice his son Isaac to prove the strength of his faith, God substituted a ram for the boy.

On the afternoon of the first day of Rosh Hashanah, there is a special ceremony called *Tashlich*, "The casting out of sins." In many places, Jews go to the banks of a river to recite the prayers asking forgiveness for their sins. The running water symbolically carries the sins away.

In the home, Rosh Hashanah is celebrated with special foods. Honey cake, and apple slices and honey are eaten, with a special blessing for a "sweet year." The traditional *challah*, or bread, is usually baked in a round shape, symbolizing the round, whole year. Sometimes challah is also shaped into a braided ladder, or decorated with birds and ladders, symbolically to help prayers rise to God and God's blessings to descend. Special delicacies are the new fruits of the fall harvest and *tsimmes*. Besides sweet potatoes, meat, and prunes, tsimmes contains carrots, whose Yiddish name is *meyrin*, meaning "to increase," as the New Year should increase in goodness.

Many Jews have adopted the modern custom of sending New Year *Shanah Tovah*, or "greeting" cards to friends and relatives. These carry the traditional greeting, *Leshanah Tovah Tikatevu*, "May you be inscribed in the Book of Life for a good year."

APPLES AND HONEY

In Israel, dates and figs join apples and honey as symbols of the sweet New Year.

Materials: Apples, honey, dates, figs, whole blanched almonds, paring knife, spoon, apple corer.

SWEET TREAT

To make a Rosh Hashanah salad or dessert, core an apple and slice it crosswise (a). *Note: Knife is dangerous and should not be used without permission or adult supervision.* Place each apple slice on a dish (on lettuce leaf, for salad), fill center with a date or fig topped with a whole almond. Drip one tablespoon of honey over all (b). Or, cut the whole apple into wedges and arrange in a circle on a dish, as shown (c). Fit a date between each wedge, and pile more dates and almonds, or figs, in center (d). Serve with honey well (following).

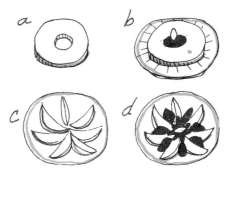

HONEY WELL

To make a decorative honey well, cut the top third off an apple. Cut a thin slice off apple bottom to make it stand upright (a). With apple corer or knife, cut a well out of apple center, leaving at least a ⅜"-thick border around edges and in apple bottom (b). Set apple on dish and fill the well with honey. Cut apple top into slices and add to another whole apple, cored and sliced. Serve slices and honey well together (c), dipping apple into honey before eating.

SHANAH TOVAH CARD

The design for this card is a scale, the zodiac sign for the months of Tishri, the season when man's future is weighed.

Materials: Card paper (all-purpose bond, or any fairly thin drawing paper or typing paper), thin wool such as baby fingering, embroidery yarn or embroidery thread, assorted embroidery needles (blunt-pointed needles are safer for young children, but sharp-pointed needles make cleaner holes), pencil, scissors, felt pen or colored pencil.

Before making your card, experiment with the wool and paper to be sure they work well together. Make a test by sewing several stitches side by side. If the wool is too thick, or the paper too stiff, or if the stitches are too close together, you will find the holes act as perforations and the sewn pieces punch out. *Note:* If the paper punches out, usually you can gently push it back in place and tape it on the wrong side of the paper, under the wool. If the piece has come completely free, you had best start again, using a thinner weight wool and/or a thinner paper, making the stitches a bit farther apart.

1. On scrap paper, practice the stitches shown. Always keep knot on wrong side of paper. To make several stitches fanning out from one point (Fern Stitch), one hole (X) may be repeatedly used.

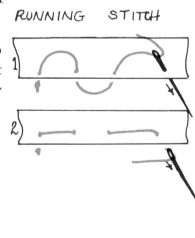

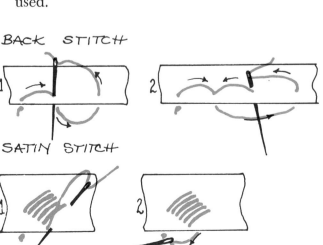

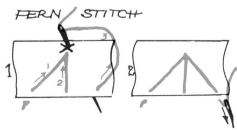

2. To make card, cut a piece of paper 9″ by 4½″. Fold in half lengthwise.

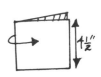

3. Trace (*see page 86*) and transfer the pattern on *page 47* to card front. Or, make up your own designs, using the symbols of Rosh Hashanah. Keep your design bold and simple. Greeting will be added later with pen or pencil.

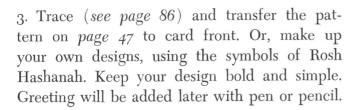

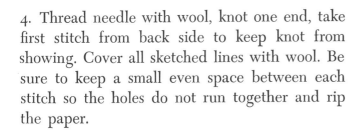

4. Thread needle with wool, knot one end, take first stitch from back side to keep knot from showing. Cover all sketched lines with wool. Be sure to keep a small even space between each stitch so the holes do not run together and rip the paper.

5. When you come to end of design, or when you want to change colors, bring wool to wrong side of paper, take at least two stitches around one of the wool loops, leave a small tail, then cut off excess. Begin second color as you did the first.

6. When embroidered design is complete, tape any punched-out areas and glue a clean piece of paper over inside of card front to hide the wool and knots.

7. With felt pen or colored pencil, write greeting on card front as shown.

YOM KIPPUR

Yom Kippur, the "Day of Atonement," falls on the last of the Ten Days of Repentance begun on Rosh Hashanah. This tenth day of Tishri (September–October) is the holiest day of the Jewish year, the day on which God examines men's lives and their repentance of the previous ten days, and writes his final decision on their future in the Book of Life, which is then sealed until the next year.

In ancient times, men commonly believed that their characteristics could be transferred to animals. On this holiday, special ceremonies were held to give the evils of men to animals, called "scapegoats." Usually, two goats were chosen and after the rites one was sacrificed and the other driven out of town. When the Temple of Jerusalem was destroyed in 70 C.E., animal sacrifice came to an end. Prayers said at that time were kept and continued, but today it is up to each individual personally to atone for his sins.

Yom Kippur is observed from sunset on the ninth to dark on the tenth of Tishri. Adults and children over thirteen fast, businesses close, and no work is done by the Jewish community, which spends the day in the synagogue. Throughout the Yom Kippur services, the rabbi and cantor wear robes of white (the color of purity) and the synagogue is decorated with white flowers.

The Yom Kippur Eve service begins with a special prayer called the *Kol Nidre,* or "all vows," chanted to a traditional melody. In this prayer, men ask forgiveness for promises to God which have been inadvertently broken. But broken promises between individuals can be mended by them alone, and this must be done before Yom Kippur.

At midday on Yom Kippur a special memorial service, called *Yizkor,* is held for friends and relatives who have died. During the afternoon service, the Book of Jonah is read from the Bible because it teaches a lesson in mercy and forgiveness. It also teaches that the presence of God is everywhere.

Jonah's story tells that God sent him as a messenger to tell the city of Nineveh that it would be destroyed because it was full of sin. To avoid this task, Jonah ran away to sea and boarded a ship. But God sent out a great storm to toss the ship, and the passengers and crew were terribly frightened. They cast lots to see who among them was to blame, and the lot fell upon Jonah. He then explained that the storm was his fault because he was running away from God. At his request, the others threw him into the sea, and at once the storm stopped. God then sent a large fish to swallow Jonah. While inside the belly of the fish, Jonah remembered God and prayed to him, and as a result was cast out of the fish onto dry land. Again God asked Jonah to go to Nineveh, and this time the humble Jonah delivered his message. The people of that city listened and repented, and because of this they were not destroyed. But Jonah was angry because his prophecy was not fulfilled. God then explained to him the importance of forgiving people who repent their sins.

The final Yom Kippur service ends with the blowing of the shofar and the greeting, *Gemar hatimah tovah,* "May you have a favorable final sealing," or verdict.

 # WHITE PAPER FLOWERS

As it is customary to do no work on Yom Kippur, these flowers should be made well before the holiday begins. Made of white crepe paper, they may be used as home decorations on Yom Kippur, or as table decorations when the fast is broken in the evening.

Materials: White crepe paper (single- or double-weight duplex), contrasting color crepe paper (for flower center), green crepe paper (single weight) or florists' tape, scissors, ruler, pencil, thin spool wire, stem wire (medium or heavy weight, *see Materials list*), rubber cement, cellophane tape.

1. To make center of flower, crush a piece of scrap paper about 8″ square into a ball about 1½″ in diameter. Stick one end of a 9″-long stem wire into ball and tape to hold (a). Cover ball with a piece of white or colored crepe paper about 6″ square, twisting ends below ball. Wrap ends with spool wire to hold (b).

2. To make flower petals, cut a strip of white crepe paper 3″ by 10″, across the grain (*arrows,* a). Fold the short end of the strip over into 2″-wide folds as shown (b). Cut folded paper into a curve (*heavy line,* c), taking care not to cut all the way down to the base. Unfold 5 petals (d).

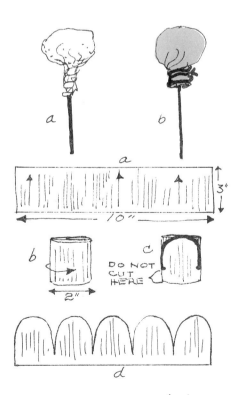

3. Spread rubber cement over bottom of flower center. Attach petals by wrapping them around base, gathering them in as they are added. Wrap petal bases with spool wire to hold them firmly to center.

4. Shape petals by pulling crepe paper across grain as shown. First, cup bottom portion of each petal as shown (a), hollowing out the area surrounding flower center. Then stretch petal tops in opposite direction (b), so they curl to the outside, away from center. If petals pull out of wire while shaping, tape at base.

5. Cut several leaves from green crepe paper, about 1″ wide and 2½″ long, grain vertical (*arrow*). Cut narrow leaf base about ½″ long for attaching to stem.

6. To cover stem, spread rubber cement over flower base and press on one end of the florists' tape (unwind it from spool as you use it) or a long strip of green crepe paper ½″ wide, cut across grain. Stretch tape or paper as you wrap, overlapping layers. *Note:* To make florists' tape stick to itself, it must be stretched and the layers well overlapped.

7. Continue wrapping stem until you reach point where leaf will be attached. Twist leaf base around stem, then cover twist with tape as you wind around it and on down to bottom of stem.

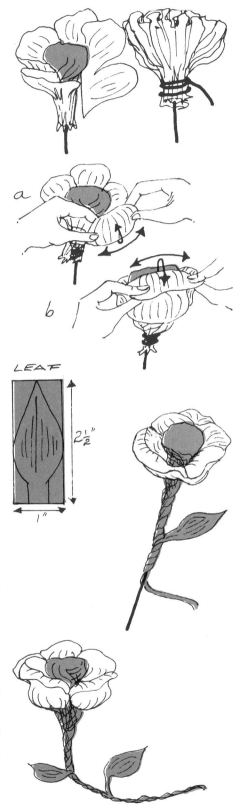

SUCCOT

At the end of the autumn harvest, on the fifteenth and sixteenth days of Tishri (September–October), the "Feast of the Ingathering," called *Succot,* is celebrated. It is believed that the festival originated with the ancient Canaanite celebration after the grape harvest at the end of the annual dry season during the autumn equinox, when rites were performed to encourage the rains. Boughs of fruit trees and evergreens were made into little booths in which the early Jewish farmers lived during this festival.

After the exodus from slavery in Egypt (*see* Pesach, *page 60*), the wandering Jews lived in tents or booths, called *succot,* pitched wherever they stopped for the night. When today we call Succot the "Festival of Booths," we remember both the ancient agricultural booths and those of the exodus.

A harvest thanksgiving festival, Succot begins five days after Yom Kippur and lasts altogether eight days. The first two are considered most holy, and many Jews do no work at this time. Families traditionally make a little booth, or *succah,* and decorate it with branches and leaves, fruits, and paper designs. It is important to cover the roof lightly, so the stars in the sky may still be seen. Special blessings are said over the fruits in the succah. In Israel today, many families eat all their meals in the succah, and sometimes even sleep there. In the city of Jerusalem, contests are held and prizes given for the most beautiful succah.

During the Succot festival, thanks are given for all growing plants by using four which have been chosen as symbolic of all the rest. These four plants are also interpreted symbolically as representative of the Jewish people. The *etrog* (pronounced *esrog*), or citrus fruit, has a good taste and a lovely smell. It stands for those people who are both educated in the Torah and who do good deeds. The *lulav,* or branch of the date palm, has a good fruit, but no scent. It symbolizes the Jew who has knowledge but no good deeds. The *hadas,* or myrtle, has a pleasant smell, but no taste, just as some people do good deeds but are not educated. The *aravah,* or willow, has neither taste nor fragrance, and stands for those people who have no education and do no good deeds. Legend tells us that God was puzzled about what to do with these varying types of people. He finally decided that they should all be tied up together with one band of brotherhood, each helping the other. For this reason, the palm, myrtle, and willow are bound together and held in the right hand, the etrog held in the left, as special blessings are said over the plants. They are then carried around the synagogue in a procession while prayers are recited for blessings on the land and fruit of Israel. In biblical times, the palm, willow, and etrog were all used in decorating the succah.

HOSHANAH RABBAH

The seventh day of Succot is celebrated as the festival of *Hoshanah Rabbah,* "The Great Salvation." A special service is held, and processions are made seven times around the synagogue. Willow branches are carried and beaten, their leaves symbols of renewed life which comes in the spring. As they are beaten, the falling leaves symbolize the arrival of rains as well as the falling away of sins.

SHEMINI AZERET

The eighth day of Succot is called *Shemini Azeret,* "Assembly on the Eighth Day." Special services in the synagogue include prayers for rain and memorial prayers for the dead.

SIMHAT TORAH

The day after Shemini Azeret is the joyous Torah festival called *Simhat Torah,* meaning "Rejoicing of the Torah." In Israel and in Reform congregations, Simhat Torah is observed the previous day, on Shemini Azeret.

Throughout the year, passages of the Torah are read aloud in the synagogue. On this day, the reading is completed, then immediately begun again, symbolizing the fact that study of the Torah has no beginning and no end. Children are given the great honor of being called to read the Torah alongside their elders; generally, only adults are called up to the Torah on other holidays and on the Sabbath. Young people also join the adults in carrying Israeli flags and specially decorated flags (which carry the greeting *Sisu vesimhu besimhat torah,* "Rejoice and be happy on Simhat Torah") in a series of seven processions, or *Hakafot,* around the synagogue. They are led by the rabbi and cantor carrying the Torahs. It is said that the procession goes seven times around in honor of Abraham, Isaac, Jacob, Moses, Aaron, Joseph, and David.

SUCCAH

This succah is small enough to be used as a table centerpiece. However, the same design may be enlarged to any size, keeping the proportions the same.

Materials: Stiff cardboard or bristol board (2-ply), green construction paper, ruler, pencil, scissors, rubber cement, paints or crayons or felt pens.

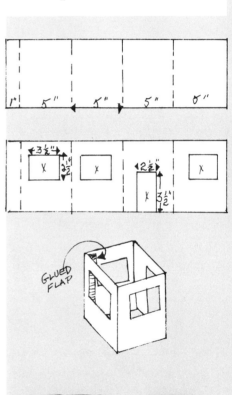

1. Cut a strip of stiff paper 21″ long by 5½″ wide. Measure, mark, and draw lines across width, dividing it into four 5″ sections with a 1″ strip at one end. Score (*see page 87*) these lines. *Note:* Scored surface is the *outside* of succah.

2. Draw windows and a door as shown (X's) and cut out these areas.

3. With pens, paints, or crayons, decorate outside and inside of succah with designs of fruits, leaves, and branches such as those shown.

4. When decorations are dry, fold up succah as shown, scored edge on outside. Glue narrow 1″ flap to inside edge of last section, closing the box.

5. To make the roof leaves, cut three strips of green paper 2½″ wide by 6″ long. Fold the short end of a strip over into six 1″ folds (a). Measure, mark, and draw a line across center of folded strip (½″ point, b). Sketch two pairs of leaves on folded strip as shown (*heavy line*, c). *Keep*

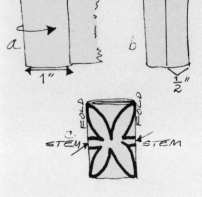

the two halves joined in the center and keep small stems touching each side at the fold. If leaves are irregular in shape, it does not matter as long as they join at center line and stems are on folds. Now, holding folded strip together carefully, cut shape out. DO NOT CUT ACROSS STEMS ALONG FOLD AND DO NOT CUT THROUGH CENTER WHERE LEAF HALVES JOIN (d). Unfold leaf strip (e). If some leaves remain uncut, cut them, but only up to stem line. Repeat for remaining two strips.

6. Note position of leaves (a). Fold up final pair (leaves 1 and 2) on both ends of each strip. Bend leaves along strip alternately forward or back from stem line, so they will look more natural when on roof.

7. Spread rubber cement over inside surface of leaves 1 and 2 (*step* 6). Press glued surface onto *outside* of roof as shown. The three strips go side by side.

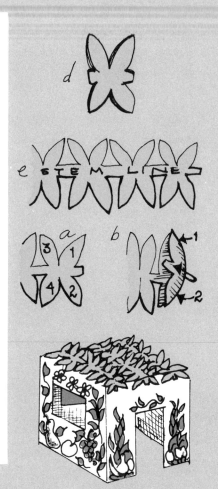

 **PAPIER-MÂCHÉ FRUIT**

These colorful papier-mâché fruits will decorate your succah or your home, and will last from year to year.

Materials: Newspapers, masking tape, wax paper, paper clips or stem wire, (medium stiff, *see Materials list*), white glue, water, 2 clean empty cans, white tempera paint, brush, brightly colored tissue paper, clear krylon spray or shellac, shellac brush, alcohol (shellac solvent), flour.

1. To make basic fruit forms, crumple newspaper into approximate fruit shapes. Wrap with strips of masking tape to hold. Fruits may be life-size or larger.

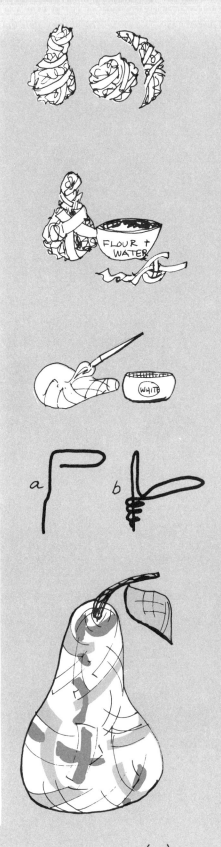

2. Spread newspaper over work area. In one can, mix water and flour into smooth creamy paste. To make papier-mâché, tear newspaper into small strips. Dip strips into paste, then smooth over paper fruit. Cover entire shape with two or three layers of this papier-mâché. Set pieces of fruit in warm place to dry until hard (at least several hours, or overnight).

3. When papier-mâché is dry, paint with white tempera paint, and set to dry.

4. To make stem and leaf, bend a paper clip as shown (a), or cut a piece of stem wire about 5″ long and bend as shown (b), into stem and leaf. Cover stem with glue (full strength) and stick it into top of fruit.

5. In second can, mix water and white glue to consistency of heavy cream. Tear colored tissue paper into small pieces, dip into glue mixture, and smooth over painted papier-mâché. To keep the colors clear and bright, do not use too many overlapping layers of tissue. Cover stem and leaf wire with green tissue paper.

6. Set tissue-covered fruit on wax paper or other smooth surface to dry. When dry (may take overnight), spray with clear krylon, or shellac to give glossy, durable finish.

(29)

SIMHAT TORAH DECORATIONS

In some synagogues, the stands of Simhat Torah flags are topped with an apple and candle decoration signifying, according to one interpretation, the fruit and light of the Torah. This decoration may also be used for a Simhat Torah table centerpiece.

Materials: One or more whole firm apples, candles (standard table size about ¾″ diameter, stubs 8″ long or less are best), apple corer, paring knife, evergreen sprigs or parsley, platter.

FLAG DECORATION

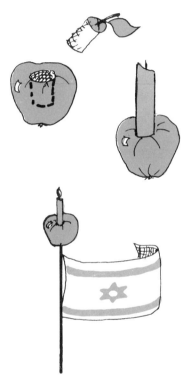

1. With apple corer, make hole in center of apple, about 1½″ deep. Be sure to leave uncut base of apple at least 1½″ thick.

2. Fit candle into hole in apple. Enlarge hole if necessary; candle should fit snugly.

3. Make Israeli flag (*see page 70*), or use traditional Simhat Torah flag, with a stand about the thickness of a wooden pencil, or larger. Stick the top point of flag stand about 1½″ into base of apple as shown. Be sure apple is firmly attached to stand, so it will not slip off. *Note:* If stand pokes up too far into center of apple, it may push candle out. If this happens, re-position stand slightly to side of apple center.

TABLE DECORATION

Follow steps 1 and 2 above. To make apple steady, cut a thin slice off apple bottom with a paring knife. (*Note: The knife is sharp and should not be used without permission or adult supervision.*) Stand apple, or group of apples, in center of decorative platter. Surround apple base with evergreen sprigs or parsley. Set platter in center of your Simhat Torah dinner table, or make one apple for each place setting at the table.

HANUKAH

Hanukah, the Hebrew word meaning "dedication," is the "Feast of Dedication," also known as the "Festival of Lights." Hanukah is celebrated for eight days, beginning on the twenty-fifth day of Kislev (November–December). The holiday honors an event which took place over two thousand years ago, when a small band of heroic Jewish men fought a victorious battle for religious freedom.

In the second century before Christ, Palestine was under Syrian-Greek rule, led by King Antiochus Epiphanes. Antiochus, sometimes called "the madman," was determined to bring all his subjects under the Greek religion. But the Jews refused to submit to him; in the village of Modin, near Jerusalem, a priest known as Mattathias, and his five sons, began a rebellion. Under the leadership of one of the sons, Judas Maccabeus ("The Hammerer"), the small band of Maccabees fought hard. The soldiers of Antiochus had overrun the Temple of Jerusalem and dedicated it to Greek gods. After about three years of fighting, the Maccabees were finally successful in driving them out and bringing peace to the land.

On the twenty-fifth day of Kislev, in the year 165 B.C.E., the Maccabees entered the Temple. They needed oil to rededicate the Temple and to light the holy *menorah,* or candelabra. A very tiny container of oil was found, and while it did not seem to be enough to last for even one day, the menorah is said to have miraculously continued to burn for eight days. For this reason, Hanukah is known as the "Festival of Lights."

Hanukah is celebrated in Jewish homes by the lighting of a small menorah and the reciting of blessings of thanks to God. Special Hanukah songs are enjoyed by the whole family. The first candle in the menorah is lit at sundown on the evening of the twenty-fourth of Kislev, when the holiday begins. An extra candle, called the *shammash,* or "servant," is also lit each night and then used to light the other candles. On the second night, two candles are lit, in addition to the shammash, and on each night thereafter, one more candle is added until on the eighth night, eight candles and the shammash are burning together. Tradition tells us that candles should be placed in the menorah from the right to the left sides, but the candles should be lit from the left toward the right.

In Israel, menorahs are lit everywhere. Tel Aviv is called the "City of Lights" at this time, because all the lights of the city are left on during the nights of Hanukah. Every public building displays its own menorah, illuminating an additional candle each night as one does in the home.

After lighting the family menorah, gifts are exchanged during each of Hanukah's eight nights. It is traditional for children to receive, among other things, little gifts of money called Hanukah *gelt.* Many years ago in Syria, a popular Hanukah gift was a candle in the shape of an upright hand with all fingers outstretched. It was believed that the hand would protect the family from bad luck and the evil eye.

Young people especially enjoy this season's Hanukah parties, with their songs and dances, delicious potato *latkes* (pancakes), and *dreydl* (top) games. The dreydl was used even in ancient times, and in places where Jews were forbidden to practice their religion, they often met to play the dreydl while they secretly prayed together. There are four Hebrew letters on the dreydl: *nun, gimel, hay, and shin.* Taken together, the letters stand for the words *nes gadol hayah sham,* meaning "a great miracle happened there," referring to the oil that lasted for eight days. On Israeli dreydls, the last letter is changed from *shin* to *pay,* which stands for the Hebrew word *poh,* meaning "here." Letters of the Hebrew alphabet also have number values, and nun equal 50, gimel—3, hay—5, and shin—300. Pay equals 80. "Put and take" games are played with the dreydl using these numbers.

Hanukah party invitations and decorations are made with the symbols of the holiday, including the menorah, candles, the Star of David, the dreydl, the hammer (Judas Maccabeus' sign), and the elephant (the animal used by the Syrian army under Antiochus).

CLAY MENORAH

This menorah should be made at least several days before the beginning of Hanukah, as it will take time for the clay to harden.

Materials: Self-hardening clay (about 1½ pounds, the type which can be used with wire armature), Hanukah candles (bought in boxes in food or stationery stores), stem wire (heavy, *see Materials list;* one piece 27″ long, four pieces 2″ long) or wire coat hanger, pliers, wire cutters, pencil, felt pen, ruler, can of water, empty clean can or paper cup, orange stick or pointed clay modeling tool, sturdy cardboard box or box lid at least 10″ square, or rotary clay modeling stand, tempera paint, brush, sandpaper or emery board, clear krylon spray or shellac, shellac brush and alcohol (shellac solvent), newspapers, felt.

1. Read directions on package of self-hardening clay. Normally, this clay requires no special preparation; it is used as it comes from the package. To keep clay moist if you must leave it for a while, cover with sheet of plastic. This clay does not need a kiln, but depending upon the size of the piece, usually dries in a couple of days at room temperature, or faster if near heat or in sun.

2. Cover work surface with newspapers. To support the weight of the clay and make the menorah stand upright, you need to make a wire armature, or skeleton. To do this, stretch out a 27″ piece of stem or coat hanger wire (you may need pliers to help bend wire). With ruler and felt pen, measure and mark off the wire as shown, starting from the right end, into sections 7″, 3″, 5″, 5″, 5″, and 2″.

3. To make base, bend the 7″ section around into a circle as shown, twisting the end under the loop to hold.

4. To make stand, bend long end of wire straight up from center of circular base and at right angles to it, as shown.

5. To make triangle, bend remaining wire up and out to the right, at point marking off the top of the 3″-high stand (a). Then bend wire to left and down, as shown (*arrows*, b) at the 5″ marks. Twist last 2″ over first leg of triangle to hold shape firm.

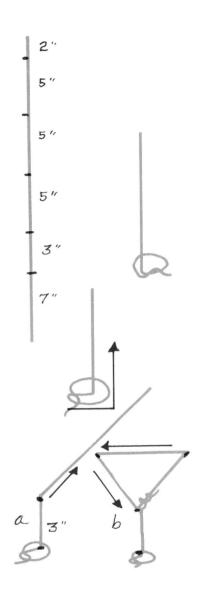

6. Place completed armature on work surface as shown. Make several rolls of clay about ⅝″ thick and press them onto wire triangle. Continue this process, pushing the wire into the *center* of the clay rolls, then with fingers and modeling tools, smoothing the clay, until entire wire triangle is covered with a smooth roll of clay ⅝″ thick.

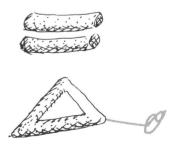

7. Make a small amount of clay "slip" in a can or cup by mixing some clay and water together until thick and creamy. *Note:* Before attaching any two pieces of clay, spread both surfaces with a little slip, then press pieces together firmly and smooth joint on all sides with fingers and modeling tool until there is no seam.

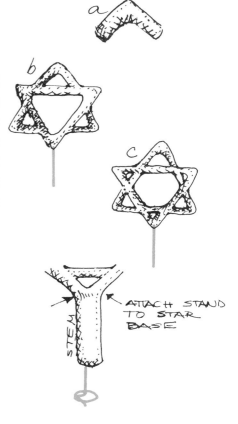

8. To complete star, model three clay rolls about 3″ long and ⅝″ thick. One at a time, bend rolls into angles as shown (a), and attach with slip in the middle of the sides of clay triangle as shown (b). Then model three rolls about 1½″ long and ⅝″ thick. Fit each roll into the corners of the first triangle as shown (c). Smooth all joints, front and back.

9. To cover stand, model several short rolls of clay ¾″ to 1″ thick and press onto stand wire. Center wire inside clay. Build clay up until stand is about 1″ to 1¼″ around and attached firmly to bottom point of star, as shown.

ATTACH STAND TO STAR BASE

10. Place box top or rotary modeling stand nearby. Add bits of clay to circular base until all wire is covered. When base is reasonably strong, carefully lift entire piece upright and stand it up on box top or modeling stand. Support star well with one hand while continuing to build up the base until it feels steady and is a circle 3″ to 3½″ across and about ½″ thick. Keeping the star on the modeling stand will enable you to view it from all sides without actually lifting or touching the clay.

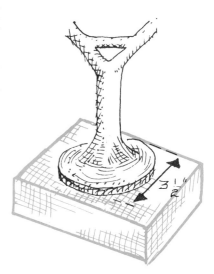

(34)

11. To add the shammash (top candle) holder, model one clay roll 1″ long by ½″ thick. Stand roll on end, gently press pencil eraser down about ¼″ into the top as shown (a). Twist and lift pencil to remove. Apply slip to base of roll and top of triangle and join surfaces. Support menorah while smoothing edges firmly (b). After holder is attached, gently replace and twist eraser to reshape hole.

12. To make remaining candleholders, cut four pieces of armature-type wire, each 2″ long. Shape four clay rolls 3½″ long and ½″ thick. Push one wire lengthwise into center of each roll. Smooth clay roll, covering wire completely. Wire is to strengthen the cross arms of the menorah.

13. Cut both ends of each clay roll with modeling tool to make rolls neat (a). Place a roll flat on table as shown. While holding it firmly, press pencil eraser ¼″ down into each end, about ¼″ in from end. Twist and lift eraser to remove (b). *Note:* Both holes must be on same side of roll. Smooth around holes with fingers. Repeat, making holes in other rolls.

14. One at a time, spread underside of each roll with slip and attach at right angles to the crosspoints of the star (*arrows*, a). Be sure to keep candle holes facing up when you attach each roll (b). Turn modeling stand or box top slowly and carefully to view star from different angles. *Add small bits of clay, with slip, around center of each roll to wedge it firmly in place in each corner.* Smooth all joints top, bottom, front and back. Be sure candle holes are still round. Supporting end of each roll so it will not bend, gently reshape any holes that need it, pushing in and twisting pencil eraser.

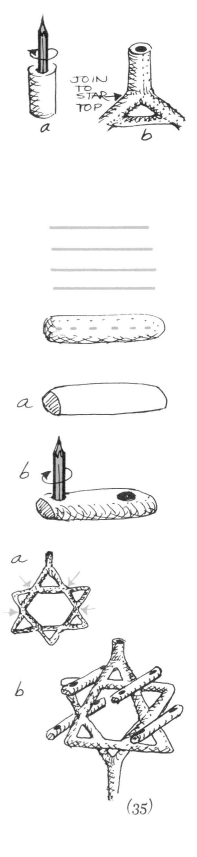

(35)

15. After all candleholders are in place, go over entire piece with modeling tool, smoothing any cracks, defining the shapes, and bending menorah into straight upright position. Stand firm, tall object (or stack of boxes, as shown) beside menorah to hold it perfectly upright as it dries. Leave on stand, set in warm place, and do not touch until dry.

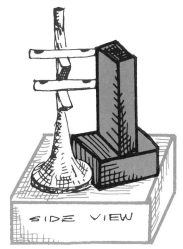

SIDE VIEW

16. Clay is dry if it clicks when tapped gently and is a light color. Smooth dry clay with sandpaper or emery board. Paint menorah with tempera paint (or spray with enamel paint). *Note:* If using more than one color, allow first coat to dry before adding second or they will run together. When paint is dry, shellac or coat with clear krylon spray for a glossy, durable finish.

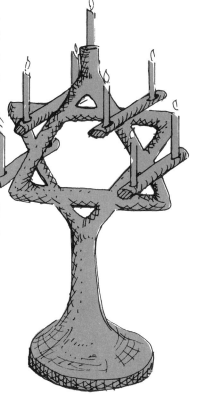

17. Cut out a piece of felt the size of bottom of circular base. Glue onto bottom of base to protect tabletop.

DREYDL BOX

This dreydl box is not only a top, but also may be used as a party favor or container for a Hanukah gift.

Materials: Bristol board (2-ply) or other stiff paper and typing paper or other flexible paper, pencil, exacto knife, ruler, scissors, rubber cement, paint or crayons or felt pens.

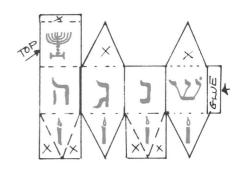

1. Trace (*see page 86*) pattern on *page 39*, and transfer to stiff paper. Cut out around all solid lines. Score all dotted lines (*see page 87*). Scored surface will be on *outside* of dreydl.

2. With paint, crayons, or pens, decorate outside of dreydl (*except areas marked X*) with Hanukah symbols such as menorah, candles, Star of David, etc. In the four central squares, draw the Hebrew letters as shown: נ -*Nun,* ג -*Gimel,* ה -*Hay,* ש -*Shin.*

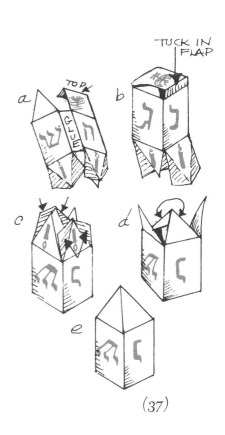

3. When decorations are dry, fold dreydl along all scored lines. (Remember, scoring is on outside.) Spread rubber cement over outside of end flap (*arrow, step 2*) and glue flap to edge of final section as shown (a). On top, fold down the two triangles and cover with square section, tucking in the narrow flap (b). Stand dreydl on table *top down.* Spread rubber cement over outside surfaces of the four folded angles (*arrows,* c). Pinch in one set of angles and press the other set on top of them, making a tent in center of box (d). Press the two side triangles onto the tent sides, completing the base (e). Add more rubber cement under triangles if necessary to make them stick firmly.

(37)

4. To make knob, cut a strip of typing (or other flexible) paper 10″ by 1″. Roll one short end over a pencil. Make one complete roll. While holding paper on pencil, brush inside of remaining strip (X's, a) with rubber cement. Roll paper tightly over onto itself, keeping edges lined up. When all rolled, slide off pencil, even edges up, and set to dry (b). Dab generous amount of rubber cement onto center of box top and onto base of knob. When glue is almost dry, press glued surfaces together (c). Top of box may be opened to place Hanukah gift inside.

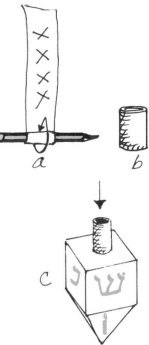

DREYDL GAMES

These traditional dreydl games may be played with your homemade Dreydl Box.

I. Each player in turn spins the dreydl, and wins the number of points corresponding to the Hebrew letter which lands upright (*see text for number values*). Highest total score wins.

II. The letters on the dreydl are also the initials of Yiddish words. Nun stands for *nikhts*, meaning "nothing"; gimel for *gants*, meaning "all"; hay for *halb*, meaning "half"; and shin for *shtell*, meaning "put in" or "add." Each player puts several tokens (dry beans, chips, etc.) in a central pot. Then each in turn spins the dreydl and, depending upon which letter comes up, they either add to, get nothing, half, or all the tokens in the pot. Player getting most tokens wins.

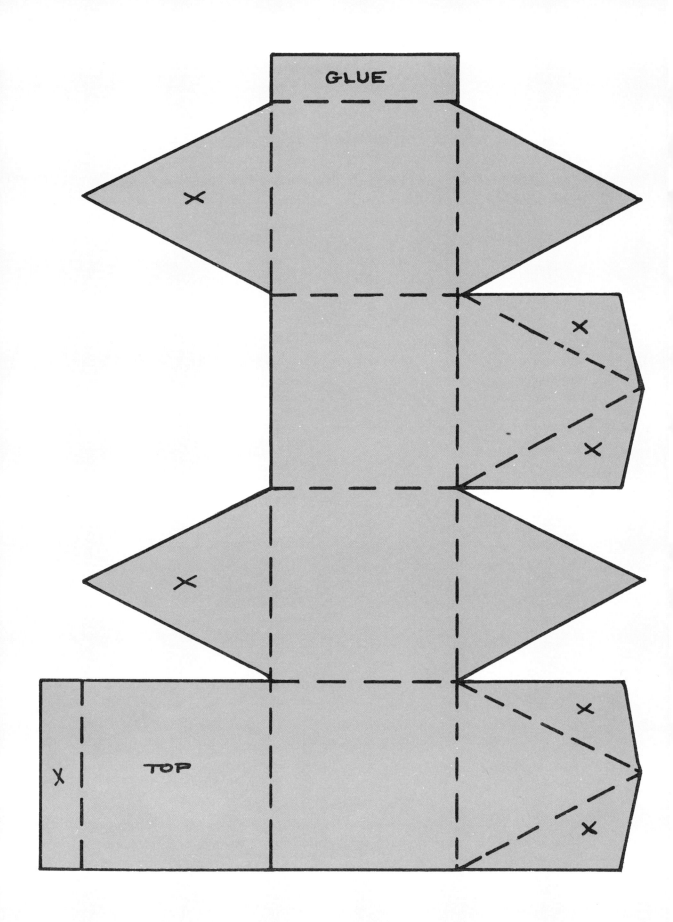

TU BISHVAT

The Israeli Arbor Day is known as *Tu Bishvat,* meaning the "Fifteenth Day of Shevat" (January–February). As Hebrew letters have number values, *tu*—15, is made up of *tet*—9 and *vav*—6. The holiday is also known as the "New Year of the Trees," or "Holiday of Planting Trees," for although it is winter in the United States, in Israel the almond trees are in bloom and the spring planting is about to begin.

Since ancient times, men around the world have understood the tree to be a symbol of strength and life. Many early customs were based on belief in the special qualities of trees. In biblical Palestine, a cedar sapling (which meant "strength") was planted at the birth of a boy. A cypress ("fragrance") was planted for a girl's birth. When children grew up and were married, their trees were cut down and used to build the *huppah,* the traditional wedding canopy.

The importance of the tree in Jewish life is illustrated by the fact that the Torah is known as the "Tree of Life." Today in Israel, the tree has an added significance. For most of the land is desert, and the existing woodlands were largely destroyed in the beginning of the twentieth century by the ruling Turks, who cut whatever wood they found to supply their new wood-burning railroad through the country. When the state of Israel was created in 1948, one of the first great tasks was the planting of trees to conserve soil, provide shade in the desert, and provide much needed wood. Since that time, over 80 million trees have been planted.

This monumental project has been accomplished largely through Tu Bishvat tree-planting ceremonies. Israeli school children travel to sites of new forests to plant small trees. There are many types of forests; for example, a children's forest, a memorial forest, and forests planted by different religious groups. The children also plant trees near their homes and schools. The Jewish National Fund, an organization devoted to helping Israel reclaim her land, helps Jews living outside Israel send money there for the buying of trees. These trees are often planted in the memory of one who has died. The Jewish National Fund also provides a means for children in foreign schools to contribute to the Israeli tree planting. A poster with a picture of a tree is given to the school or class-room. Beside the tree are many "leaf" stickers which the students "buy" for a small contribution and paste onto the tree. When the tree is full of leaves, enough money has been collected to buy a tree. The poster and money are then sent to Israel where a tree is planted in the children's name.

In Israel, schools which plant the most trees are given prizes at ceremonies which include plays about the meaning of Tu Bishvat. Children wear handmade evergreen wreaths in their hair, and the decorations are made of tree boughs. Israeli fruits such as figs, dates, almonds, raisins, pomegranates, and *boksor* (fruit of the carob tree) are traditionally eaten during Tu Bishvat in recognition of the fact that it is an agricultural festival. In ancient times, it was the custom to taste at least fifteen different types of fruits, because the festival is observed on the fifteenth of the month.

Decorations for this holiday might include illustrations of Israeli trees such as the cedar, cypress, eucalyptus, tamarisk, carob, pistachio, gopher, walnut, almond, olive, apple, pear, orange, grapefruit, lemon, and apricot, or such typical Israeli flowers as the cyclamen, narcissus, or anemone.

 # TU BISHVAT TREE POSTER

This tree poster will help you collect money to buy and plant a tree for yourself, your family, club, or class. Before making the poster, inquire at a tree nursery and decide what type of tree you wish to buy, how much it will cost, and how many contributions of what size you will need. For example, if you need three dollars, and your group has thirty people, you will need thirty contributions of ten cents each (divide the number of people into the total cost). When you make the tree, draw as many leaves as you will need contributions (thirty).

Materials: Poster paper (one standard-size sheet, about 22″ by 28″), tempera paints and brush or crayons, felt pens, etc., jar or box for collection of money.

1. On poster paper, sketch a large tree as shown. This is a stylized, rather than realistic, tree. On the branches, draw as many leaves as you need contributions (*in example, thirty*).

2. Paint or color trunk, branches, and green leaf area *behind drawn leaves*. DO NOT PAINT IN LEAVES; keep them blank.

3. As each contribution is received, the contributor paints one blank leaf green. The blank leaves remaining show you how much more money you need. When the tree is completely green, you have enough money to buy your tree.

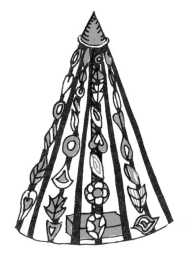

TU BISHVAT TREE

This decorative tree may be made in any size, depending upon the time and effort you wish to put into its creation. A paper tree is quicker to make, but a felt and wool tree is more unusual and more durable. Before starting the project, decide which material you will use. The large tree used in the example below may be made by several people working together. Realistic looking leaves may be copied from picture books of Israeli flowers and trees, found in a library. Or, create your own imaginative leaf and flower designs.

Materials: Cardboard tube (fairly stiff, gift wrapping paper tubes are best, 26″ long, 1¼″ diameter), cellophane tape, cardboard box (should have close-fitting top, may be a stationery or note-paper box, about 3¾″ by 4¾″ by 3″), pencil, ruler, scissors, masking tape, plasticene clay, green felt or green paper, felt or paper of various other colors, crayons or tempera paints or felt pens, wool (of various colors and thicknesses), white glue, rubber cement, stapler, stem wire (medium stiff, *see Materials list*, 2 lengths each 27″), stiff cardboard, chalk, spray starch (optional).

TREE

This tree can be made in any size; simply use the general proportions given in the example below.

1. Prepare the box to be tree's base. First, make a hole in box lid. To do this, stand one end of 26″-long cardboard tube in *center* of box lid as shown, and draw around it (a). With exacto knife (*which is dangerous and should not be used without permission or adult supervision*) or scissors, cut out hole (b).

2. Push tube through hole in lid. With piece of masking tape, attach lid lightly to tube's center. This will keep lid out of the way until needed. *Note:* Top of lid faces top of tube.

3. Measure and mark off points 1″ from each end of tube. Make 4 or 5 evenly spaced cuts in each end of tube up to 1″ marks. Fold cut flaps outward as shown.

4. Find center of inside bottom of box. Spread rubber cement in 2″ circle over *center* point. Also spread rubber cement on *under* sides of *bottom* tube flaps. Press glued surfaces together (*arrows,* a), so tube stands straight up inside *center* of box. Before glue is completely hard, remove tape and slide lid down until it fits over box bottom. If tube is on center, lid should close easily (b); if tube is off center, lid will not fit. In this case, lift lid and slide tube until it is centered and lid will close. Then slide lid back up to tube center and retape.

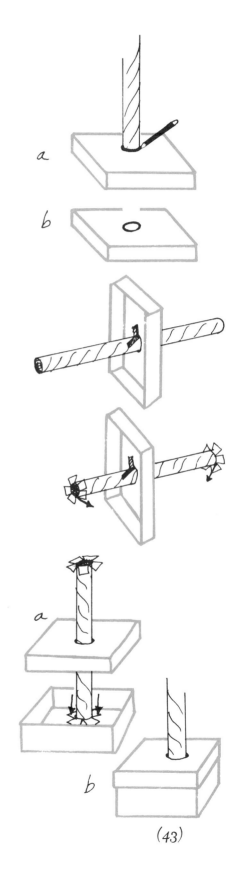

5. To make base stable and keep tree upright, box bottom will be filled with plasticene clay. To begin, firmly press small bits of clay over glued tube flaps. Add clay until flaps are well covered and stuck to box bottom. Continue to fill box with packed clay until box is weighted down and will not tip over. (*Note:* Instead of clay, box may be lined with tinfoil and filled with plaster of paris; *see page 64.*)

6. Remove masking tape, slide lid down, closing box. Now paint tube and entire base green, or cover with glued-on green paper.

7. Cut a disc of stiff cardboard slightly larger than tube top with flaps spread out (about 5½″ in diameter). When tree is complete, this disc will form the top.

8. Tree branches are made from strips which will be attached between the cardboard disc and a wire hoop. To make hoop, bend two pieces of stem wire 27″ long into a circle. Twist ends together. Hoop is about 14″ in diameter. *Note:* Hoop may also be made of a ½″-wide, 54″-long strip of cardboard stapled together to make circle 14″ across. If stem wire or cardboard is not green, hoop may be covered by winding on green florists' tape or green crepe paper strips.

LEAVES AND BRANCHES

Leaves and branch strips may be made out of paper or felt. Whichever material is used for leaves should also be used for branch strips.

1. To determine length of felt or paper branch strips, measure from tree top to 2″ above base bottom (22″). Then add 1½″. Cut twenty felt or paper strips 23½″ long and about ⅝″ wide.

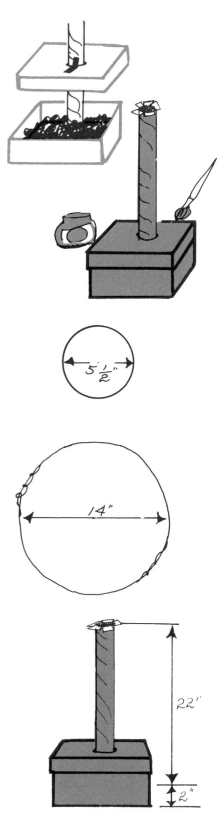

2. Staple about ½" of each strip to edge of card board disc as shown. Strip ends should be almost side by side.

3. Spread out flaps on tube top. Cover top surfaces of flaps with rubber cement (X's, a). Spread rubber cement on *center* of *underside* of cardboard disc. Press glued surfaces together, centering tube on disc bottom. To hold tube flaps firmly, tape them to disc with cellophane tape (b).

4. Place hoop (*Tree, step 8*) on flat surface. Stand tree base in center of hoop. Spread strips out evenly as they hang from disc. Working first with four strips at opposite points, attach them to hoop by pulling end of each strip over hoop, then up about 1" on underside and stapling it to itself (a). Using same method, attach other strips between these four points (b).

5. Leaves may be made from either paper or felt decorated with wool. Whichever material is used, cut some leaves smaller and narrower for tree top, others longer and wider for bottom area. *Leaves are attached to every other strip around tree.* Leaves vary from 1½" to 3" wide and 3" to 4" long; six leaves fit on each of ten alternate strips, so sixty leaves are used altogether.

a. Paper Leaves

Trace (*see page 86*) leaf patterns on *page 47*. Transfer to fairly stiff colored paper (such as construction paper), and cut out. Repeat until you have enough leaves of varying sizes. Decorate leaves with crayons, tempera paints, or felt pens. Staple finished leaves to front of alternate paper branch strips, or glue on with rubber cement.

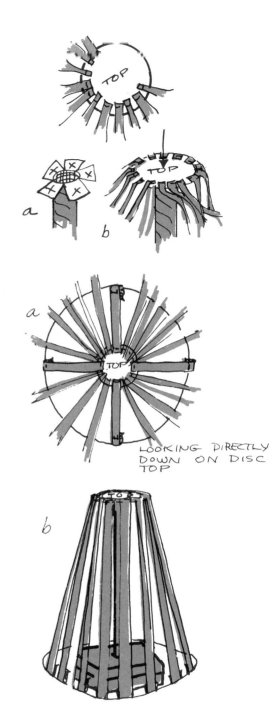

LOOKING DIRECTLY DOWN ON DISC TOP

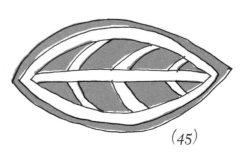

(45)

b. Felt and Wool Leaves

Trace (*see page 86*) leaf patterns on *page 47*. Transfer to stiff paper and cut out. Place on colored felt, hold down (or pin to hold) and draw around outline with chalk or pencil. Cut shapes out. Repeat until you have enough leaves of varying sizes. (*Note:* At this point, felt leaves may be stiffened if desired by spraying with spray starch, then ironing dry.)

To decorate, first lightly sketch design lines on felt with chalk or pencil (a). Outline design contours with thin line of white glue. Press lengths of colored wool onto glue (b). Wool may be poked into place with embroidery needle, pencil point, or paper clip, as fingers quickly tend to get sticky. Set leaves aside to dry; glue is not visible when dry. Glue backs of leaves to front of alternate felt strips with rubber cement.

6. To finish tree top, cut a green paper or felt circle about 9″ in diameter. Remove a wedge 7½″ across (a). Overlap ends and glue (paper) or staple (felt) together into cone. Cut ½″ flaps all around base of cone (b). Supporting disc on tube top, spread ½″-wide strip of glue (heavy line) over edges of disc top (c). Fold paper cone flaps under, spread bottoms of flaps with glue (X's, d); felt will not fold easily, so spread glue on flaps as shown (e). Bending flaps under, press cone, point up, onto tree top, covering stapled branch strips. Finished cone is about 3½″ high. If cone is felt, glue piece of wool about 18″ long around edge of cone base, to finish neatly (f). Paper cone may be decorated with paint or covered with glued strips of wool.

(46)

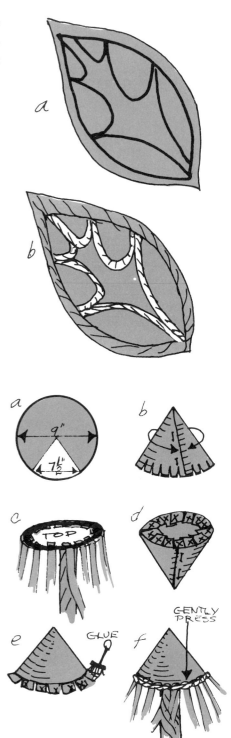

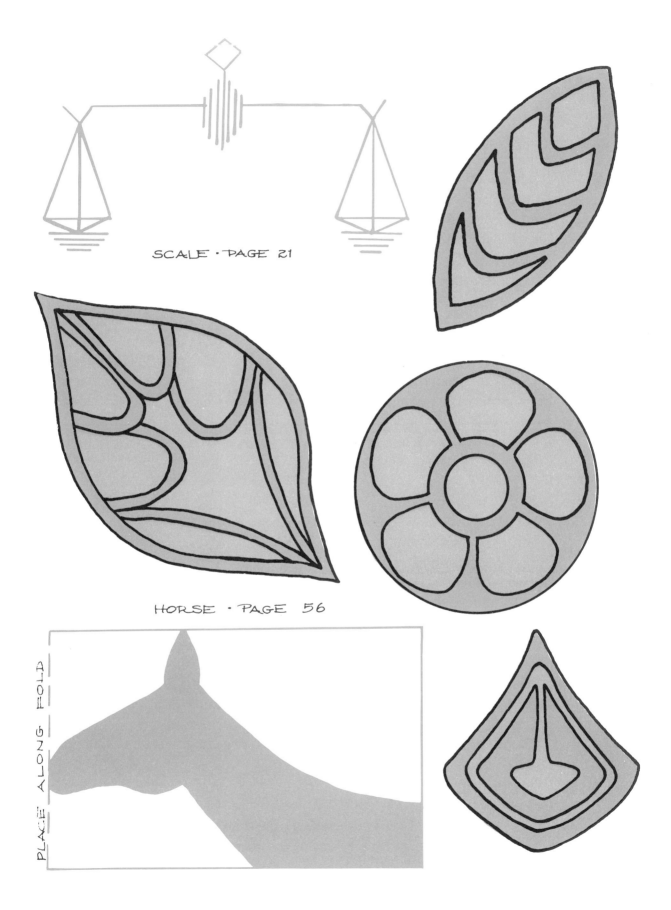

SCALE · PAGE 21

HORSE · PAGE 56

PLACE ALONG FOLD

PURIM

Celebrated on the fourteenth day of Adar (February–March), *Purim* is known as the "Festival of Lots." However, the origin of the word "purim" is uncertain. It is thought by some to come from a Persian word, *pur*, meaning "lot," although no such word exists in either the Hebrew or Aramaic languages spoken by the Jews of Persia. It may well derive instead from the Arabic word *phur*, meaning "New Year," and the holiday itself may have its origin in the ancient Persian New Year festival.

In the synagogue, Purim is celebrated with the reading of the *Megillah*, or Book of Esther, from the Bible. We learn that in the fifth century B.C.E., the Persians, under King Ahasuerus, ruled lands in which the Jews lived. During a banquet one evening in his palace in Shushan, King Ahasuerus sent for his Queen, Vashti, to show her beauty to his male guests. Vashti refused to come, and the King, enraged and afraid other women might follow her bold example, had Vashti removed from his court. He then decreed that as a matter of law, wives could never again disobey their husbands. To choose a new queen, Ahasuerus held a contest to find the loveliest young girl in the kingdom. The winner was an orphan named Esther (Hadassah). Although she did not tell him, Esther was a Jewess, and her cousin and guardian was the Jewish leader, Mordecai.

Soon after Esther became queen, it happened one day that Mordecai overheard two servants plotting to kill the King. He told Esther, who warned the King in Mordecai's name. At the King's command, it was written into the books of the kingdom that Mordecai had saved the King's life.

At this time, the King was under the influence of his favorite minister, a wicked man named Haman, who hated the Jews. Haman wished to have everyone in the kingdom bow respectfully before him, and the King issued a decree forcing them to do so. The only man who refused to bow was Mordecai, who explained to the furious Haman that he would bow in humility only before God. In his rage, Haman made plans to kill Mordecai and all his people. He cast lots (*pur*) to determine which day the Jews should be killed, and chose the thirteenth day of the twelfth month, Adar. Haman then went to the King and persuaded him to send orders to all the ministers in the kingdom ordering them to kill all Jews on this day.

When Mordecai heard of the King's plan, he sent word to Esther that she must try to save the Jews by persuading the King to change his mind. Esther asked Mordecai and all the Jewish people to give her strength by observing a three-day fast. The determined young Queen then invited Haman and the King to join her at a banquet. That night at the banquet, the King asked Esther to tell him what she most desired. In reply, she invited the King and Haman to a second banquet.

Returning home full of pride from the first royal supper, Haman passed Mordecai, who once again refused to bow to him in the street. At once, all Haman's joy was turned to blind hatred; he returned home, and with his wife Zeresh and several of his friends, devised a plan to prepare a gallows from which to hang Mordecai.

That same night, the King could not sleep. To pass the time, he asked that the records of the kingdom be brought in and read to him. By chance, the story of Mordecai's saving the King's life was read, and the King, recalling the brave deed, was shocked to find that no special honor had yet been paid to this man. At that moment, Haman entered the court, having returned to ask permission to hang Mordecai. Finding Haman there, Ahasuerus summoned him, asking his advice: "What shall be done unto the man whom the King delighteth to honor?" And Haman, naturally thinking that *he* was to be honored, replied that such a man should be clothed in the King's own robes and crown and paraded in honor through the streets of the city riding the King's personal horse. "Make haste," said the King, ". . . do even so to Mordecai the Jew." Thus, the stunned Haman was forced to honor his enemy, parading him triumphantly through the streets of Shushan, announcing to all that Mordecai was a man much honored by the King.

The next evening Haman and the King again joined Esther at a banquet. Again the King, charmed by her graciousness, offered Esther whatever she wished. The clever Queen had planned carefully for this moment, and at the King's request, boldly answered that she was Jewish, and that her people had been condemned to death by the wicked Haman. Aghast, the King fled from the table into the garden, while the terrified Haman threw himself at Esther's feet to beg for mercy. Returning, Ahasuerus saw Haman thus, and thought he was about to attack the Queen. At this, he sentenced Haman to die on the same gallows he had prepared for Mordecai. Esther was given all Haman's property, and Mordecai his position as the King's minister.

At the King's bidding, Esther and Mordecai wrote a new order, decreeing that Jews throughout the kingdom had the right, and royal permission, to fight and defend their lives on the thirteenth day of Adar, when they would be attacked. For, by custom, the original royal decree could not be reversed, though a new one could be issued. Horses, mules, and camels carried messengers with the new order throughout the kingdom, and the Jews rejoiced.

Fighting broke out on the thirteenth of the month, and lasted two days. The Jews were victorious, and on the fifteenth day they rested, feasting and celebrating. So it was that the fourteenth day of the month of Adar was proclaimed a holiday, to be forever more celebrated as the festival of Purim. The thirteenth of Adar is observed by fasting and is known as the Feast of Esther.

Children as well as adults attend the Purim service, and in an atmosphere of great merriment and even greater noise, they boo, hiss, and wave *greggers* or *klappers* (noisemakers) whenever Haman's name is mentioned. In some places, Haman's name is chalked on the soles of the feet, which are then loudly stamped at the appropriate moments during the reading of the Megillah. Uninhibited gaiety is an important Purim tradition, expressed by the word *adloyada*, from the Hebrew phrase *ad lo yada* meaning "Till he did not know" (what was happening).

In Israel, elaborate Purim carnivals are held. Tel Aviv, for example, has a festive three-day celebration called Adloyada which features parades, parties, and dramatic presentations. Masquerading is one of Purim's favorite customs, enjoyed by Jews throughout the world. At Purim parties and masquerade balls, costumes represent the principal figures in the story of Queen Esther. Contests are held to choose the most beautiful Esther, the most wicked Haman, and the most dignified King. Adults as well as children enjoy the plays and puppet shows retelling the Purim story. In many Jewish communities, particularly in Persia and Israel, effigies, or dummies, of Haman are paraded and finally burned in bonfires. Both masquerading and the burning of effigies were common activities of the ancient Persian New Year celebration.

Mishloah Manot or *Shalak-mones*, the exchanging of gifts, is a popular Purim custom. In Israel, children always make the presentation of the gift for the family. The most common gifts are special holiday foods, including poppyseed candy and the traditional *Hamantashen*, or "Haman's pockets," which are triangular pastry envelopes filled with poppyseed or prune-nut mixtures. During Purim, gifts are also made to charities, in remembrance of Mordecai's wish that the Purim celebration include the poor.

PURIM FINGER PUPPETS

If you wish to write your own puppet show, the preceding story of Purim may be elaborated upon, or you may prefer to go back to the original, adapting your own text from the Book of Esther in the Bible. You will find professionally written plays in your public or synagogue library.

AHASUERUS   ESTHER   MORDECAI

HAMAN   SERVANT   HORSE

BASIC PUPPET FOR ALL CHARACTERS

Materials: Flexible (shirt) cardboard, colored paper, masking tape, scissors, ruler, pencil, stapler or needle and thread, rubber cement, colored pencils or felt pens or crayons, colored wool or raffia, scraps of fabric (assorted sizes), trimmings (such as ribbon, lace, feathers, old costume jewelry), colored foil.

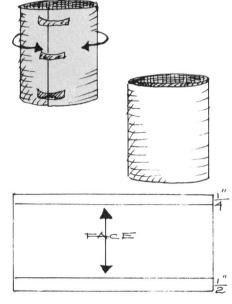

1. To make puppet head, cut strip of flexible cardboard 2¼″ by 4½″. Roll strip around your finger into a tube about 1¼″ across. Overlap ends and wrap with masking tape to hold.

2. To cover tube, cut a strip of flesh-colored paper 2¼″ by 4½″. Wrap paper around tube and while holding it there, lightly mark the central area on front where puppet's face will go. Seam is in back.

3. Place paper strip flat on table. Lightly mark lines ¼″ down from top and ½″ up from bottom as shown. Face will fit between these marks. In example, we will make King Ahasuerus; for other faces, *see page 51.*

4. With felt pens, crayons, or colored pencils, draw puppet's face in marked area. For hair, beard, moustache, etc., indicate with pencil lines where you will want to glue wool. Wool is added later. When features are complete, wrap paper around tube, overlap ends and glue firmly.

SIDE VIEW

5. To make hair, beard, and moustache, measure and cut strips of wool the length of your pencil-drawn hair. Short pieces for forehead, full-length pieces to cover entire back of head. Glue on strips. For beard, cut wool as long as you like, but only apply glue above the ½″ line on tube, so robe can be attached below this point. Beard will hang down over robe front.

6. To make puppet's robe, cut a circle of fabric 10″–12″ in diameter, or a rectangle about 9″ by 12″. Fold fabric in half (a), then in quarters (b). Cut a small (about ¾″) piece off corner marked "X" (b). Open fabric (c) and enlarge hole if necessary until it *just* fits over bottom end of cardboard tube.

7. To attach robe, spread rubber cement over outside surface of the clear ½″ wide band on base of puppet's neck. Turn head upside down. With fabric *wrong side up,* fit hole over tube and press fabric edges onto glue.

8. Cut short strips of masking tape and cover edges, pressing half tape onto cloth, the other half onto inside of tube.

9. Turn tube head up and fold down cloth as shown.

10. Place hand inside puppet, middle finger inside head, other fingers arranged as shown. Mark points where the two "arm" fingers stick up (*arrows,* a). Remove puppet from hand and cut holes in marked arm points large enough for fingers to stick through (b).

11. For suggested puppet costumes, *see page 51.* Trim the robe with ribbons, gold braid, lace, shawls of fabric bits, etc. For Esther's bracelets, make several colored foil rings and wear them along the length of the fingers which make Esther's arms. Cut King Ahasuerus' sceptre (*see page 51*) out of colored paper or foil and glue or sew it to his robe.

(53)

CROWNS AND HATS

Ahasuerus

1. Cut a strip of foil or decorative wrapping paper 5¼″ by 1½″. Sketch points in top half as shown, then cut out.

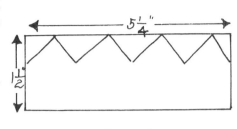

2. Decorate by gluing on bits of beads, feathers, etc.

3. Wrap crown snugly around top of puppet's head and mark where overlapping ends meet. Glue or staple ends together at this point. Place crown on Ahasuerus' head (*see illustration, page 51*).

Esther

1. Cut a strip of foil or decorative wrapping paper 5¼″ by 1½″. In strip's center, sketch trefoil design (X) as shown, with middle peak touching top of strip. On both sides of trefoil, sketch shorter petal shapes. Cut out design.

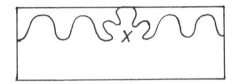

2. Decorate by gluing on bits of beads, feathers, or bits of colored foil, especially in center of trefoil.

3. Finish as in Ahasuerus' crown, *step 3*.

Mordecai

1. Cut a strip of decorative paper or fabric 5¼″ by 2″. Spread strip lengthwise and fold up ⅓ of width as shown (a). If hat is paper, make several vertical cuts in top ⅔ of width (b), so folded brim will stand slightly away from top of hat when completed.

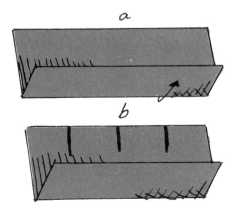

2. With folded edge on bottom, wrap hat snugly around puppet's head and mark where over-

lapping ends meet. Staple, glue, or sew ends together at this point. Place crown on Mordecai's head (*see illustration, page 51*).

Haman

1. Cut a strip of black paper 5¼″ by 2½″. Draw a line lengthwise across top of strip about ½″ down from edge (X).

2. With ruler against top edge of strip, mark off center (A) of strip (2⅝″ from each end). Then mark off points B and C, each 1⅝″ out from center point A.

3. At points A, B, and C, make short cuts into top border, just as far down as line X.

4. Fold cut flaps down over line X. Flaps are top of hat.

5. Fitting one short flap inside the other, wrap hat snugly around puppet's head. Mark where overlapping ends meet. Remove hat and glue or staple ends together. Place hat on Haman's head (*see illustration, page 51*).

Other Men and Servants

1. Cut a strip of paper or fabric 5¼″ by 2″.

2. Place strip lengthwise on table, then make a cone by folding ends toward center and down, overlapping them as shown (a). Fold overlapped ends up as shown (b), making hat base even all around.

3. Holding folded ends together as shown (2–b), fit hat onto puppet's head, spreading or closing cone base until hat fits snugly. Remove hat and staple, sew or glue ends together as shown. Place hat on puppet's head (*see illustration, page 51*).

(55)

HORSE (OR OTHER ANIMAL)

1. Make basic head tube, follow *step 1, page 52*. Cover tube with brown paper as in *step 2, page 52*.

2. To make horse's head, cut strip of brown paper 2½″ wide by 8″ long. Fold short ends over in half (2½″ by 4″). Trace pattern (*see page 47*) and transfer to folded paper, placing nose on fold (a). Holding both halves of paper together, cut shape out (b). DO NOT CUT THROUGH NOSE FOLD.

3. With paper flat, add eye on each side, and nose and mouth using colored pencils, felt pens, or crayons.

4. Open both halves out and place *face down* on table. Spread rubber cement over both halves of neck (X's).

5. With nose in front (a), press glued necks to each side of tube, overlapping and gluing ends in back. Bottom of ears are level with tube top. Be sure to note that neck slopes *downward* on tube, so head is raised (b).

6. With scissors, carefully trim away back of tube top (*dotted area*, a) beginning behind ears and following neck line. To make mane, glue bits of wool or raffia over forehead and across tube top and down onto each side of neck (b).

7. Make robe out of brown or black fabric as in *steps 6–9, page 53*.

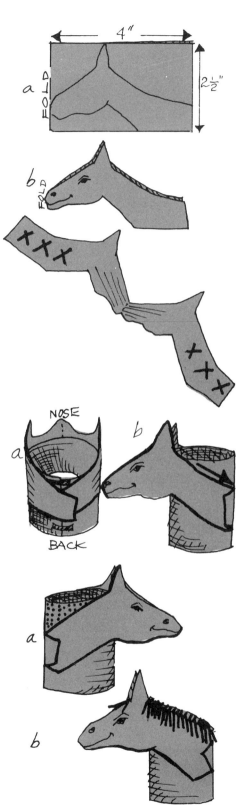

(56)

MONLACH

  Poppy-seed Candy

These popular Purim candies are known as *monlach,* from the Yiddish word *mon,* meaning "poppy." The poppy seeds may be combined with almonds, or with any other type of nuts.

Ingredients: ½ pound (1⅓ cups) poppy seeds
1 cup honey
1 cup slivered blanched almonds
½ teaspoon powdered ginger
cooking oil
(Makes about forty 1½″ squares.)

Equipment: Measuring cups and spoons, medium-size saucepan, wooden spoon, cookie sheet or marble slab, sharp knife, spatula, boiling water, sieve, mixing bowl.

1. Use oil to grease cookie sheet or marble. Set sieve over mixing bowl. Measure poppy seeds into sieve, cover with boiling water. Drain seeds and repeat once more. Set seeds aside.

2. Measure honey into saucepan. Stirring continually, bring to a boil over medium heat.

3. Add poppy seeds and almonds to honey. Continue to stir, keeping mixture at slow boil until very thick (about 5 minutes). Spoon a few drops of mixture onto greased sheet. If it holds its shape and is not at all runny, mixture is thick enough.

4. Stir in ginger. Then turn mixture out onto greased sheet. Oil back of wooden spoon and pat mixture out into a rectangular shape about ⅜″ thick. (If you allow mixture to cool a few minutes, you can oil your hands and pat candy out on sheet.)

5. When spread mixture has cooled slightly (about 5 minutes), use sharp knife (*which is dangerous and should not be used without permission or adult supervision*) to cut it into 1½″ squares. If knife sticks, dip it in hot water.

6. Cool candy until hard (at least one hour). Remove pieces to platter with spatula. To make candy crisp, chill in refrigerator before serving. Individual pieces may be covered with clear plastic wrap.

 MOTHER'S HAMENTASHEN

The addition of lemon gives this traditional Hamentashen recipe a delightful flavor and keeps the prune filling from becoming too sweet.

Pastry ingredients:
2 eggs
½ cup sugar
¼ lb. (1 stick) melted butter
2 tablespoons water
1 teaspoon vanilla extract
1 lemon (rind grated, pits removed, and pulp grated or chopped)
½ teaspoon baking soda
½ teaspoon baking powder
pinch of salt
3 cups flour (more or less)

Filling ingredients:
12-ounce can (1¼ cups) prune "butter" or pastry filling (or same quantity of cooked, pitted prunes put through food mill)
1 lemon (rind grated, pits removed, and pulp grated or chopped)
½ cup coarsely chopped walnuts
½ cup crushed Corn Flakes
cooking oil
honey

Equipment: Mixing bowls, measuring cup and spoons, grater, table knife, large spoon, teaspoon, cup or small bowl with mouth 3½″ to 4″ in diameter, wax paper, rolling pin, cookie sheets, wire whisk or egg beater, spatula.

(Recipe makes about 2 dozen Hamentashen.)

1. Set oven to 375°. Grease cookie sheets with cooking oil and set aside.

2. Make pastry dough first. Beat eggs in mixing bowl. Then beat in sugar, butter, water, and vanilla. Add grated lemon rind and pulp.

3. Sift baking soda, baking powder, salt, and flour and add to above mixture. Mix together until dough forms a ball and seems stiff enough to be rolled out. Add a little more flour if necessary to make dough workable. Wrap dough in wax paper and refrigerate while making filling..

4. To make filling, place canned or milled prunes in mixing bowl. Add grated lemon rind and pulp (pits removed). Add chopped nuts and crushed Corn Flakes and mix well.

5. Remove dough from refrigerator. Set a portion of dough on a lightly floured piece of wax paper (about 15″ long). Rub small amount of flour onto surface of rolling pin, then roll out dough until quite thin (less than ⅛″ thick).

6. To cut circles of dough, turn bowl or cup upside down and press its rim firmly into rolled dough (a). Twist bowl, then lift, leaving cut circle (b). Repeat, making circles as close together as possible all over rolled dough. Peel away excess dough between circles and add it to remaining dough. *Note:* If bowl rim sticks to dough, dip rim in flour.

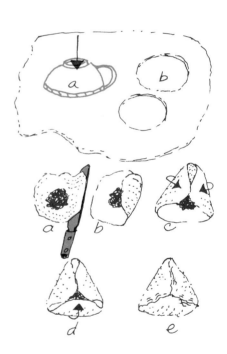

7. Place one full teaspoon of prune filling in center of each dough circle. Then slip table knife under one edge of dough circle as shown (a), and flip side of dough over filling (b). Repeat on two other sides (c and d), making triangular envelope. Pinch all seams of dough, sealing filling inside (e). Repeat *steps 6* and *7* to use up remaining dough and filling.

8. Place Hamentashen on greased cookie sheets. Leave a little space between them as they expand slightly when baked. Drip ¼ to ½ teaspoon of honey over the top of each. Bake until golden (about 12 minutes) at 375°. With spatula, remove to platter.

PESACH
(Passover)

Pesach, or Passover, the "Festival of Unleavened Bread," was traditionally observed for seven days, from the fifteenth to the twenty-first of Nisan (March–April). Today, only the Jews of Israel and Reform Jews of other countries celebrate it for seven days; Orthodox and Conservative Jews celebrate for eight days, with special observances on the first two days. One of the most important of all Jewish holidays, the roots of Passover reach far back into history.

Canaan was the ancient name of the Middle Eastern region which later came to include Palestine and Syria. The people of this fertile area west of the Jordan River were primarily agricultural. To protect their crops of figs, grapes, wheat, and barley, they worshipped local gods called *baalim,* and held seasonal rites to honor the sun, moon, and rain. These gods were known to the earliest wandering tribes, and thus their memory was carried into Egypt by Jacob and his twelve sons when they migrated from Canaan. The enslavement of the Hebrew tribes in Egypt is believed to have occurred under Pharaoh (King) Ramses II, who lived from 1299 to 1232 B.C.E. It was during the time when his successor Merneptah, came into power that Moses led the Hebrew tribes out of slavery, out of Egypt. During this period of coming out, or exodus, from Egypt, and through their later wanderings, these people chose one of their gods, Jehovah, as their own, the source of all their inspiration. With their migration into Palestine (at the time of the Iron Age, about 1200 B.C.E.), Jehovah replaced the local baalim and became the God of Israel. The new religion emphasized the idea of *one* god, and the elaborate temple ceremonies developed in his honor evolved into Judaism, whose basic laws had already been set down by Moses when he received the Ten Commandments from God on Mount Sinai.

As the ancient agricultural festivals were adapted by the Hebrews, they were explained in terms of the new religion. Two of these, *Pesach* and *Mazôth* had been celebrated in the spring, at the time of the full moon nearest to the spring equinox. At the Pesach ceremony, a lamb was sacrificed, originally representing an offering to the god of fertility, the moon-god. The blood of the lamb was then used as a sign, to ward off evil spirits.

Mazôth was celebrated at the barley harvest, near Pesach time, and as part of the ritual, only unleavened, flat bread could be eaten for one week. On the second day of this week, a measure of the new barley crop, called an *omer,* was presented to God as an offering.

These two ancient holidays were combined in the Jewish religion, and given additional meanings in terms of the exodus from Egypt, which had occurred at the same time of the year. This is seen in the name of the early festival, Pesach, which in Hebrew meant literally "skipping" or "gamboling"; after the exodus, the word was reinterpreted to mean the "skipping over" or "passing over" of Jewish homes by the Angel of Death. Thus, today, Pesach means "Passover."

According to tradition, God sent two messengers, Moses and his brother Aaron, to beg the Egyptian Pharaoh to free the Hebrew people from slavery. He refused, and as punishment, God sent ten plagues down upon the Egyptians: water turned to blood; frogs; lice; wild beasts; cattle disease; skin disease; hail; locusts; and darkness. Though Egyptians (and Jews as well) suffered throughout these nine, Pharaoh would not soften. The tenth plague was the death of the firstborn male child in every family. For protection, the Jews smeared lamb's blood on the doorposts of their homes. Because of this sign, the Angel of Death "passed over" every Jewish house, killing only the Egyptian children. The Egyptians were stunned by their children's deaths, and as Pharaoh was himself a firstborn son, he was frightened for his life. He called for Moses and Aaron and ordered them immediately to lead the Jews out of Egypt.

On the fifteenth day of Nisan, the Jewish people rushed to leave, taking their bread dough without waiting for it to rise. Later, during their flight, they baked the flat, unleavened bread in the hot desert sun. Although they were grateful to be free from slavery, the Jews were afraid Pharaoh might soon change his mind and send soldiers after them. It was not long before this happened, and the Jews found themselves trapped between the advancing Egyptians and the Red Sea. It was then that a miracle is believed to have occurred: God divided the waters, allowing Moses and his people to cross the sea on dry land, then closed the gap to drown the pursuing Egyptian army. Every year since, Jews throughout the world have celebrated Passover as a festival of freedom, recalling their escape from slavery in Egypt and confirming the fact that every man has the right to be free.

Matzoh, "unleavened bread," is eaten during Passover in memory of the flat bread eaten by the Jews during the Exodus. No leavened (risen) food (in Hebrew *chomets*) is permitted in a Jewish home during this holiday. To rid the home symbolically of the chomets, a ceremony is held before Passover begins, in which crumbs of leavened bread are placed on a windowsill. They are then swept with a feather into a wooden spoon, a blessing is said, and the next morning the crumbs are burned, cleansing the home for Passover.

On the first two evenings of Passover, the primary activity is a special feast called a *seder,* meaning "order," because a particular order is followed. During the seder, the *Haggadah* (from the Hebrew word *l'hagid,* "to tell") or story of the Exodus is read. In stories, prayers, psalms, and songs, the Haggadah explains the historical and religious meaning of the holiday. The seder is designed to be especially interesting for children. So that they do not get bored, they are often allowed to crack and eat the nuts which are traditionally served. They participate in the service by asking the "Four Questions" about the seder customs. In answer, the father reads from the Haggadah, explaining all the symbols found on the table.

The special "seder plate" contains a roasted lamb bone and a roasted egg, symbolizing the ancient paschal sacrifices; *maror,* or bitter herbs (horse-radish), symbolizing the suffering of the Jews while slaves in Egypt; *haroset,* a mixture of wine, chopped apples, and nuts, representing the mortar which the enslaved Jews used to make for the Pharaoh; salt water, symbolizing their tears while slaves; and *karpas,* a green vegetable such as parsley or celery, symbolizing hope and new growth in the spring. An extra goblet of wine placed on the table is known as the "Cup of Elijah," for when the door is momentarily opened during the service, it is believed that the good prophet Elijah will come inside, sip from the wine, and herald the coming of the Messiah. It is true that the wine can often be seen moving in the glass, and who can say whether the table has been nudged or Elijah has arrived? During the seder, one drinks four cups of wine, each symbolizing a promise made by God to help the Israelites in Egypt. Of the three pieces of specially wrapped matzoh on the table, part represents the "poor bread" eaten in Egypt, and part is hidden secretly by the head of the family. The hidden piece is called the *afikomen,* from the Greek word meaning "dessert," and the children who search and find it after the Haggadah is completed at the end of the seder, "sell" it back to their father for a small gift. This custom is said to be the world's oldest treasure hunt. In medieval Europe, it was believed that the afikomen had special powers as a charm. Some Jews kept a piece hanging in their homes all year to guard against the evil eye and fire. Moroccan Jews are said to have calmed stormy seas by throwing a piece of the afikomen overboard during a voyage. The seder ends with the reciting of riddles and the singing of traditional songs such as *Had Gadyah,* "An Only Kid."

SEDER PLACE CARDS

These decorative cards will show your guests where to sit at the seder table. They will also remind you of the important Passover symbols.

Materials: Colored construction paper or other fairly stiff paper, scissors, pencil, ruler, exacto knife, crayons or felt pens.

1. To make card, cut paper 3½″ by 3½″. With ruler, measure, mark, and draw a light pencil line dividing paper in half (1¾″).

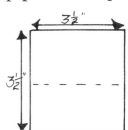

2. In the center of card, (line horizontal as shown) sketch a design of one of the Passover symbols (wine goblet, matzoh, pyramid, parsley, shank bone, characters in song *Had Gadyah*, etc.). Allow about half the design to stand *above* the center line as shown, but it should stop about ¼″ from top edge of card.

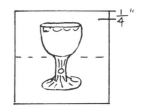

3. With crayons or felt pens, color design. When dry, use exacto knife (*which is dangerous and should not be used without permission or adult supervision*) or scissors to cut around outline (green line) of design sticking up above center line.

4. Lightly score (*see page 87*) center line from outside edge up to beginning of each side of design. DO NOT SCORE ACROSS DESIGN.

5. Fold top half of card down and back, leaving design (goblet) standing straight up. *Note:* For some designs, you may want to glue on bits of lace, buttons, feathers, leaves, etc.

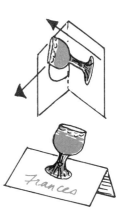

6. Write guest's name below design and stand place card on seder table.

SEDER TABLE CENTERPIECE

The paschal egg and the growing tree branch of spring are the main elements in this decoration as they have special significance on Passover, when one hopes for a new start and a happy, free future.

Materials: Eggs (six or more, whole and white), sewing needle, bowl, scissors (narrow-tipped manicure scissors and regular shears), thread, drawing paper, green tissue paper, rubber cement, pencil, paints or crayons, paper towels, plaster of paris (*see Materials list*), one large empty can for plaster, one clean empty can (6-ounce size) with top removed or small flowerpot with hole inside taped closed, water, branch of tree, or shrub such as lilac (about 14″–16″ tall), colored ribbon or gold braid (about ¼″ wide) or thin colored wool, empty egg carton, green tissue paper.

1. If branch is picked several weeks before the start of Passover and set in water in a warm place, it will start to bud by the beginning of the holiday. If you use a budding branch, set it in water in an attractive and stable pot or vase and proceed to *step 5* to decorate with eggshells.

2. If you cannot pick a branch in time to have it bud, use the bare branch as it is. (If you prefer to color it, branch may be sprayed with green or other color enamel.) Bare branch will be set in a base of plaster so it will not tip over when on table; also, painted and plaster-based branch may be used from year to year.

To prepare plaster, measure (measurements are for base of 6-ounce juice can) about ¾ cup water into large can. Slowly sprinkle about 1⅔ to 1¾ cup plaster on top of water, mixing with your hands. Squish plaster and water together, adding more plaster as needed until mixture is almost as thick as soft ice cream. Pour mixed plaster into can (or flowerpot), filling to within about ½″ of top (a). Set container of plaster aside for a few minutes until it begins to set—you can tell when the time is right because branch stem will stand up unsupported in center of plaster (b). Leave branch standing up in center of plaster and do not touch until plaster is completely hard (at least two hours).

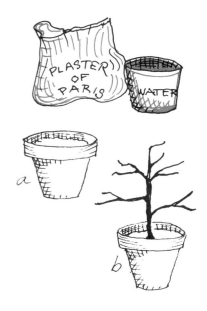

3. To cover outside of can, spray with enamel paint or cut a strip of colored paper, wrap it around can, and glue ends together. Flower pot may be decorated by gluing on strips of colored ribbon or braid or wool.

4. To add leaves to bare branches, cut green tissue-paper leaves of various shapes with one end tapered as shown (a). To attach leaves, apply rubber cement to tapered end and wrap it around branch (b). Or, make leaves suggested on *page 45* or *46* sewing thread loops onto leaf tops for hangers.

5. To make eggshell decorations, first blow the eggs. This is done by making one small hole about ¼" across in the pointed, narrower end of the egg, and another hole slightly larger in the side as shown. Hold egg over bowl, side hole down, press your lips to top hole and blow contents of egg into bowl.

6. Rinse and dry each eggshell. Draw a light pencil oval around side hole of each egg as shown.

7. To cut out oval, place tips of manicure scissors into side hole, then make short little cuts out in a spiral (a). Keep cuts short and use only scissor tips or the shell will crack. When you reach pencil line, try to cut a clean unbroken edge (b). Small cracks may be repaired by spreading rubber cement on inside surface with fingertip. (If egg is still sticky, rinse and blot dry.)

(65)

8. Cut strip of ribbon or braid or wool about 7″ long and glue around outside surface of cut-out oval as shown. This will cover uneven edges.

9. Thread needle with 8″ length of thread. Pull needle up in center and tie both ends of thread together in double knot (a). Cut a piece of paper about ¼″ to ⅜″ square. Stitch up through center of paper, then slide paper down to rest on knot (b). Place needle inside shell and stitch out through top hole, pulling thread up gently until paper catches on inside of shell and covers hole. Cut thread just below needle, tie ends of thread together making loop from which egg will hang (c). Set aside eggs with hangers in an egg carton or other safe place while preparing interior designs.

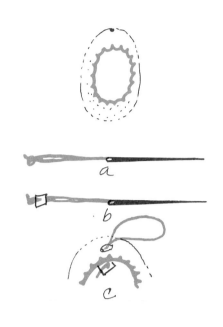

10. Using colored paper, pipe cleaners, bits of ribbon or whatever imaginative combinations of materials you can find, make small design of the Passover symbols, such as those illustrated (a). You might also use a shank bone, pyramid, the characters in the song *Had Gadyah*, etc. Total height of the design should be about 2″, including a ½″ stem which is folded under (b) and glued down inside egg bottom (c). With felt pen or paints, the outside of the shell may be decorated with the Hebrew name for whatever object is inside the shell.

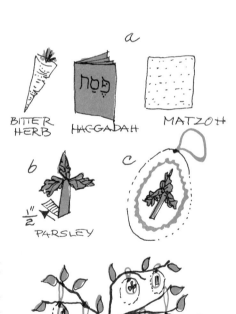

11. Hang eggshell decorations by their thread loops, arranging them evenly about the limbs of the branch. Set decoration in center of your seder table. The shells will turn with the movement of the air.

YOM HA'AZMAUT
(Israeli Independence Day)

More than two hundred years after Judas Maccabeus rededicated the Temple of Jerusalem (*see* Hanukah, *page 31*), it was destroyed by the Romans, in the year 70 C.E. The destruction of the Jewish population of Palestine began at this time, and was completed with Bar Kokhba's defeat before the Roman armies in the year 135 C.E. (*See* Lag B'Omer, *page 75*). Although Jewish communities spread through the world and continued to grow, for more than eighteen hundred years the Jewish people dreamed of returning to their homeland and rebuilding their Temple.

In the nineteenth century, Jewish leaders, spurred on by growing anti-Jewish feeling in Europe, began a movement called *Hibat Zion,* or "Love of Zion," urging Jews to move back into Palestine. In 1897, a Viennese journalist, Dr. Theodor Herzl, founded the World Zionist Organization, which actively interested many Jews in the establishment of a Palestinian homeland. Before the end of World War I, the World Zionist Organization was successful in persuading the British Government to issue the Balfour Declaration, so called because it was signed, on November 2, 1917, by the then Foreign Secretary, Lord Arthur James Balfour. This Declaration stated that the British Government favored, and would help with the building of, a Jewish national home in Palestine. During this time, many Jews from all over the world moved back into that country. As Jewish Palestine grew, with its modern agricultural and industrial developments, so the Arab residents' fear, opposition, and hatred of the Jewish immigrants grew.

As the British army had captured Palestine from the Turks, and was already there, it agreed to facilitate the settling of Jewish immigrants. However, the British more often than not sided with the Arabs against the Jews, and slowly increased restrictions against the Jewish rights of immigration, land purchase, and settlement. Because the British police and army favored the Arabs, a Jewish defense organization developed during this time called the *Haganah,* meaning "self-defense." During World War II, Jewish soldiers fought in all the allied armies against Hitler's Germany. Many Haganah members fought in the British army, and some were formed into a special force for the defense of Palestine, called the *Palmach,* or "shock troops." By the end of the war, in spite of the Balfour Declaration, British restrictions against the Jews had grown into forceful opposition. The desperately sad survivors of the Nazi concentration and extermination camps were forced to try to *sneak* into Israel, protected from the

British army, navy, and police only by night's darkness and the brave Haganah. Many of these immigrants were not only turned away from the Israel they had just barely lived to see, but some eleven thousand were once again put into concentration camps, this time by the British on the Mediterranean island of Cyprus.

This conflict between Jews, Arabs, and British finally reached the attention of the world, and a United Nations Commission was appointed to study the problem. The Commission proposed that the British Mandate, or rule, of Palestine be ended and the country be divided into separate Arab and Jewish states. On November 29, 1947, the United Nations voted to accept this partition of Palestine, thereby creating a legal Jewish state.

At this decision, Arab violence against the Jewish communities grew, for they felt threatened and feared displacement. Surrounding Arab countries, including Syria, Lebanon, Transjordan, and Saudi Arabia threatened the Jews with war as soon as the British troops left the country. The Proclamation of the State of Israel was made by the provisional, or temporary government, headed by David Ben-Gurion, on May 14, 1948. On this day, the Declaration of Independence of the new country was read. On the next day, May 15, British troops left and the country was immediately attacked by armies of seven Arab countries. The Haganah defense organization became the Israeli army, and brilliantly defended its new homeland. During this "War of Liberation," the Arabs were defeated, and many Arab residents of the new Jewish state fled, creating what has become a major refugee problem. On the twenty-fourth of February, 1949, Egypt, then Lebanon, Transjordan, and Syria all signed an armistice, or truce, with Israel, ending the war.

On January 25, 1949, the first *Knesset*, the Israeli Parliament, was elected and David Ben-Gurion became Prime Minister of the new government. On May 11 of that year, Israel was admitted to the United Nations.

Israeli Independence Day, the fifth day of Iyar (April–May), is observed by Jews throughout the world, but the celebration is most meaningful in Israel. The twenty-four hours preceding the holiday are observed as Memorial Day. This is a solemn time, including five minutes of silence through the entire nation in memory of those who died in the defense of Israel. Special memorial services are held. The next day, a brilliant joyful celebration breaks forth, with parades, singing, dancing of *horas* (traditional circle dances), and parties. In major cities such as Tel Aviv, stages are set up in public squares, and entertainers organized by the city government perform for the assembled crowds. Israeli flags, menorahs (the state symbol), and the Israeli coat of arms are displayed as decorations.

TISHA B'AV

The fact that the Jews now have a home in Israel is a source of joy and inspiration. Prayers are said for the continued strength and survival of Israel on *Tisha B'Av*, the "Ninth Day of the Month of Av" (July–August). Hope for the future is the one bright aspect of this day, one of the saddest in the Jewish calendar. It is the day to remember, with fasting and mourning, the most tragic events which have occurred in Jewish history. On this day more than twenty-five hundred years ago, in the year 586 B.C.E., the first Temple of Jerusalem, built by King Solomon, was destroyed by the Babylonians. They took the Jewish people into captivity, but those Jews who later returned built a second Temple. This Temple was destroyed by the Romans, led by General Titus, on the ninth day of Av in the year 70 C.E. Again the Jews were exiled from Palestine. In the year 1492 C.E., the same year Columbus discovered America, the Jewish people were expelled from Spain on the ninth day of Av.

In the synagogue on Tisha B'Av, the Ark containing the Torah, or Holy Scriptures, is draped with a black cloth. Hymns are sung in mournful tones and sad prayers are recited. People sit on low benches and pray with their heads bent low. It is a day to recall past sadness; but it is also a day to hope for the future.

ISRAELI FLAG

CARDBOARD PRINT

A single Israeli flag print may be attached to a stand as described below, or a decorative flag chain may be made from several prints. Placing them side by side, staple one short end of each flag over a length of string, making a gay Independence Day decoration.

Materials: White drawing paper 8″ by 11″, cardboard (one stiff piece 8″ by 11″ for base, other pieces flexible enough to be cut with scissors—shirt cardboard or corrugated cardboard), glue, ruler, pencil, scissors, blue tempera paint, brush, shellac (optional) and brush, alcohol (solvent for shellac), stick or dowel 16″ long and about ¼″ diameter, stapler, wooden spoon, paper towels, cellophane tape.

1. Mark the 8″ by 11″ cardboard base as shown. Top space A is ¾″, top band B is 1½″, center space C is 3½″, bottom band D is 1½″, bottom space E is ¾″. Mark the center point of whole flag (X), 5½″ in from ends and at a point 4″ between top and bottom edges.

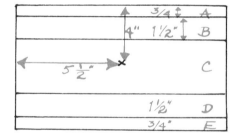

2. Cut two strips of flexible cardboard, each 8″ long and 1½″ wide (a). Measure, mark, and cut out (see note at right, b) two cardboard triangles on which all sides are 3¼″ long and ¼″ wide.

CUT IN HERE TO REMOVE CENTERS

3. In their marked areas (B and D), glue down the two long strips as shown.

4. Center the triangles around point X, gluing down one triangle first, then gluing the second over it, as shown.

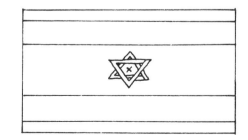

5. If you plan to print many copies of your flag, the entire surface of the cardboard should be shellacked when the glue is dry. For up to five copies, you do not need shellac. Wait until shellac is dry before proceeding to *step 6*.

6. Have drawing paper nearby. Prepare thick, not watery, paint. Brush an even layer of blue tempera paint over all *raised* surfaces on cardboard. Try not to get paint on background.

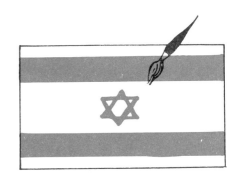

7. Now working quickly, place white paper directly over cardboard, lining edges up. DO NOT SLIDE PAPER. Holding paper down firmly with one hand, rub all over it with fingers or back of wooden spoon. You will be able to see through the paper somewhat; be sure you have rubbed over entire *raised* design.

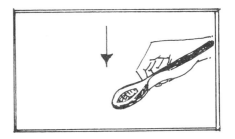

8. Peel off paper. Do not let it slide or print will blur. To make more prints, repeat *steps 6 and 7*. With damp paper towel, wipe off any extra paint that gets onto background areas. Dry cardboard before making next print. When finished printing, wipe paint off cardboard with paper towel.

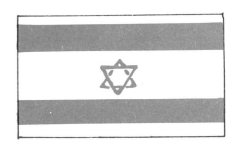

9. When flag print is thoroughly dry, it may be attached to stick or dowel. Mark off point 1½″ from one end of dowel (a). Immediately below this mark, glue or tape on one short end of flag. To glue flag, turn it face down on table and spread ½″-wide strip of glue down one short edge, then wrap glued strip around dowel just below 1½″ mark. From front, glued flag looks like this (b).

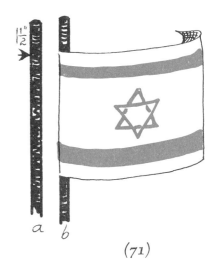

ISRAELI COAT OF ARMS

The seven-branched menorah is the symbol of the State of Israel. On the coat of arms, the menorah is surrounded by the olive branches of peace and the word *Yisroyel,* "Israel" in Hebrew. The menorah stands upon a base of six blocks in order to form a design of seven elements. The importance of the number seven in ancient numerology is probably due to the fact that each phase of the moon lasts about seven days (*see page 12*). This string and bean print of the Israeli coat of arms may be used for a wall decoration or an Independence Day party invitation.

Materials: Stiff cardboard (rectangular in shape and at least 8½″ by 11″), medium thick cotton string, dried beans, scissors, white glue.

1. Trace pattern on *page 72,* and transfer (*see page 86*) to cardboard rectangle. Or, sketch your own design on cardboard.

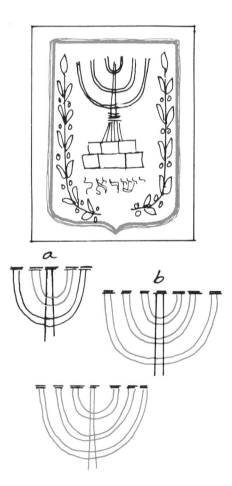

2. Cut three pieces of string, each 32″ long. Spread glue around shield border and press on the three rows of string side by side, covering lines.

3. To cover curved arms of menorah, first cut two pieces of string, one 4″, one 5″. Spread glue over lines of smallest "u." Press shortest string over top curve, longer string over bottom curve. Strings should be about ¼″ apart (a). Then cut two more pieces of string, one 6½″, one 7″. Press these onto glue covering the middle "u." Remember, shortest string goes on upper line. Last, cut two strings, one 8¼″, one 9¼″. Cover bottom "u" (b).

4. Cut two pieces of string 3½″ long. Glue over vertical lines forming central arm and stem of menorah as shown. Go right over curved arms.

5. Cut fourteen pieces of string about ⅜″ to ½″ long. Glue two of these pieces side by side at the top of each arm as shown.

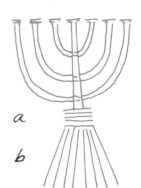

a

b

6. Cut five pieces of string about ¾″ long and glue horizontally, side by side at base of menorah stem as shown (a). Cut eight pieces of string 1″ long and glue on vertically just below cross pieces, completing stem (b).

7. Cut three pieces of string 3¼″ long and glue onto lines forming the top three boxes of stand. Then cut three pieces of string 4″ long and glue around bottom three boxes. Spread inside of each box with glue and press down as many dried beans as will fill each area.

8. Cut two pieces of string 8¾″ long. Glue one down the length of each olive branch. Then cut twenty-six pieces of string 2″ long and glue each piece onto a leaf. At the bottom of each pair of leaves, glue down two dry beans as shown.

9. To write the Hebrew word *Yisroyel,* wind bits of string around each letter, cut correct length, and glue down over lines. Or, draw or paint letters on finished print.

10. When all glue is dry, complete print following directions on *page 71, steps 6–8. Note:* After printing, string-bean design on cardboard may be shellacked and kept as a decorative piece of art work.

LAG B'OMER

The festival of *Lag B'Omer* is closely related to both Pesach (*see page 60*) and Shavuot (*see page 83*). In biblical times, Passover was celebrated near the time of the barley harvest. It was then the custom, on the second day of Passover, for farmers to bring to the Temple an offering of one *omer* or measure of newly ripened barley. On that day, according to the law of the Torah, would begin the counting of the omer, or forty-nine days between Passover and Shavuot, which was the fiftieth day. These *sephirah,* or "counting" days are still marked by Jews, who at sundown recite a special blessing counting the passage of each day: "Today is the——day of the Omer. . . ."

Thus, Lag B'Omer means "Thirty-third day of the counting of the Omer." The day is so named because, as Hebrew letters have number values, Lag stands for the number thirty-three (*lamed*—30, *gimel*—3). The observance takes place on the eighteenth day of Iyar (April–May).

During the course of Jewish history, several events which took place during these "Counting Days" are celebrated on Lag B'Omer. The Jews of the ancient Palestine area had long lived under the rule of the Roman Empire. From time to time, when this rule was felt to be insupportably unjust, they revolted. But the reign of the Emperor Hadrian, in the year 114 C.E., at first seemed to be fair enough to the Jewish people. Then, in the year 132, the Romans made plans to establish their own colony in Jerusalem, dedicating the Jewish Temple to Roman gods and forbidding the Jews to continue the practice of their religion. Under the leadership of the wise Rabbi Akiba, the Jews made preparations for a rebellion. Their officers were largely Rabbi Akiba's pupils, under the command of Bar Kokhba. In the course of the war, a plague killed many of the students of Rabbi Akiba. On the thirty-third day of the Omer, the plague miraculously stopped. In honor of these student-soldiers, Lag B'Omer is called the "Scholar's Holiday." The army of Bar Kokhba fought well, and for a long time succeeded in keeping the Romans out of Jewish lands. But finally, the Romans sent Julius Severus, one of their strongest generals and the ruler of Britannia, to crush the rebellion. In the year 135 C.E., the Romans defeated the Jews.

During this same period of harsh Roman rule, Jews were forbidden to teach their religion. But one great rabbi, Rabbi Shimon Bar Yohai, disobeyed the Romans and continued to teach. Eventually, he was discovered and forced to flee. With his son, Eleazar, he hid in a cave for twelve years, living solely on the fruit of a carob tree and the water of a spring which miraculously appeared beside their cave. Young students would come to the country each day to see the rabbi, carrying bows, arrows, and picnic baskets to fool the watching Romans. Only after Emperor Hadrian's death did the rabbi and his son leave their cave, on the thirty-third day of the Omer, returning home to teach the Torah. When he died, Rabbi Shimon Bar Yohai was buried in the village of Meron, in northern Galilee. Today, Jews of Israel go to his grave, as they did centuries before, to celebrate Lag B'Omer as the "Feast of Rabbi Shimon Bar Yohai" with singing and dancing around a bonfire. At this time, Orthodox Jewish children three years old are given their first haircuts, while visiting the grave in Meron.

In honor of the Scholar's Holiday, Jewish school children in the United States as well as in Israel, go on picnics, build bonfires, fly kites, and play with bows and arrows.

LAG B'OMER AIM GAME

As a substitute for archery, this aim game may be played at your Lag B'Omer party or picnic. In honor of the fact that this is the Scholar's Holiday, you will learn both the number values and the Hebrew letters that make up the words Lag B'Omer.

Materials: Seven empty, clean tuna fish cans (or other cans of similar size) with tops removed, 12 paper clips, tokens (dried beans or macaroni or small pebbles), colored paper, scissors, rubber cement, crayons or felt pens, stiff cardboard or box lid.

1. Cut strips of colored paper wide enough and long enough to wrap around outsides of six cans. (Uncovered can will go in center, *step* 3.) Decorate outside of each strip with Lag B'Omer symbols such as those shown at right. Wrap each paper around a can, overlap, and glue ends to hold.

לג בעמר

LAG B'OMER

2. Place can on paper, draw around outline of bottom. Repeat seven times. Cut out circles of paper large enough to cover inside bottom of each can (seven circles in all). With brightly colored crayon or felt pen, draw the Hebrew letters and their number values in each of six circles as shown. In the seventh circle, write "double score." This circle goes inside the uncovered can. Glue circles (letters up) inside cans.

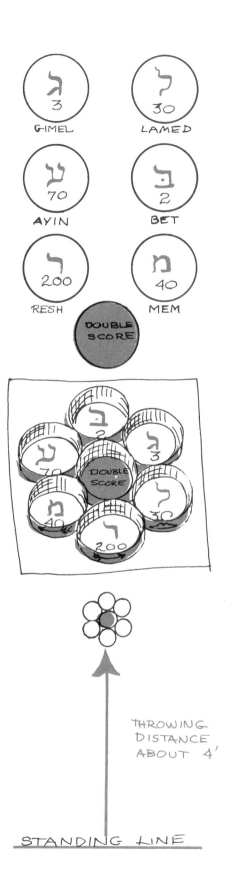

3. On a piece of stiff cardboard, arrange cans in circle as shown, with sides touching. Uncovered can goes in center. Paper-clip sides together at dots.

4. Carefully lift cardboard containing cans and place it about 4' or more away from a standing line. Each player gets six tokens. In turn, each throws the tokens into the cans. The score is determined by adding the number values from each can in which the tokens land. If *one or more* tokens land in center can, total score is doubled. For example, if three tokens land in outer circle cans, in *lamed*—30, *bet*—2, and *mem*—40, and one token lands in center can, score for that play is 72 doubled or 144. Highest score wins.

 **LAG B'OMER KITE**

Decorate your kite with colorful designs, and use it for a wall decoration when it is not in flight.

Materials: 30″ by 36″ piece of tissue paper, plastic sheeting or gift wrapping paper (comes in roll 30″ wide), two balsa wood sticks (each 36″ long, ⅛″ thick, and ¼″ wide or ⅜″ thick by ⅝″ wide), rubber cement, pencil, medium thick white cotton string (at least 30 yards long; some flyers use string as long as 100 yards), round stick (about 12″ long, 1″ thick), scissors, ruler or yardstick, cloth rags or old sheet, exacto knife, masking tape, crayons, colored felt pens or tempera paints and brush.

1. Place 30″ by 36″ sheet of paper *right side down* on work surface. All working lines will be drawn on wrong side which is now facing up. Arrange paper as shown, with short ends at top and bottom. With ruler or yardstick, measure, mark, and draw a line across width of paper 10″ down from top edge (A). Then measure, mark, and draw a line (B) down length of paper, dividing it in half (15″ from each side).

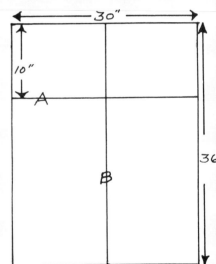

2. Using straight edge of ruler or yardstick, draw lines as shown, connecting both ends of line A with both ends of line B. This makes basic kite shape.

3. Measure, mark, and draw dotted lines 1″ inside kite outlines. This will be a fold line.

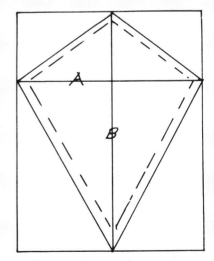

4 Along line A, measure and mark off points 2″ in from angles C and E. Then draw lines from these points (perpendicular to line A as shown) to outside edges of kite. Along line B, measure and mark off a point 2″ down from angle D and 3½″ up from angle F. Then draw lines perpendicular to line B as shown.

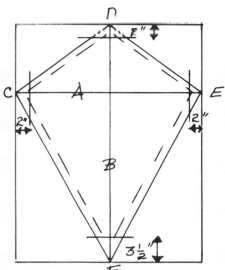

5. Cut around outlines of kite (a). Cut off each angle along lines drawn in step 4 (b).

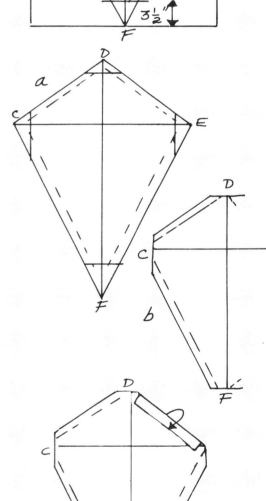

6. Again place kite *right side down* on work surface. Carefully fold edges over along dotted lines as shown. Keep fold right on line, or size of kite will vary and it will be unbalanced when flying.

(79)

7. Turn kite *right side up* and decorate with paints, crayons, or felt pens. Or, make a collage by cutting out designs of colored paper and gluing them down. Designs may be flowers, trees, smiling sun face (as shown), bows and arrows, Star of David, or Hebrew word Lag B'Omer (*see page 76, step 1*).

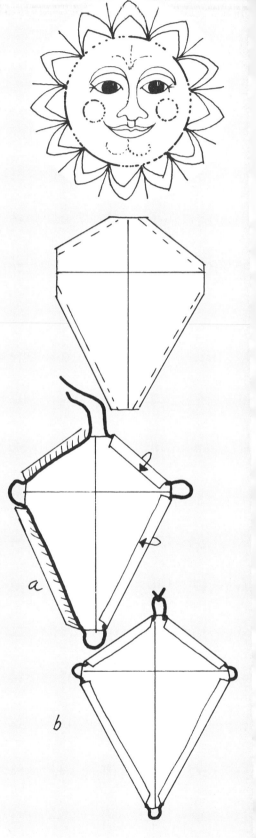

8. When decorations are dry, place kite *right side down* on work surface. Cut piece of string about 90″ long. Spread a ½″-wide line of glue on inside edge of folded strip (as shown, yellow lines) and on kite body, ½″ away from fold line. This leaves a clear space about ½″ wide along both sides of fold line.

9. With both ends of string at kite top as shown, arrange string inside folded edges, leaving a string loop about 1″ long sticking out of each angle. Push string all the way back inside fold, along dotted line, then bend folded edge over and press glued surfaces together (a). String is covered and should be exactly along outlines of kite. *Note:* If glue has been correctly placed, string will slide, so you can pull it gently until all angle loops are the same size. Then tie the two loose ends together in double knot, making top loop same size as others (b). Cut off extra string above knot.

10. Cut balsa sticks as follows: With exacto knife (*which is dangerous and should not·be used without permission or adult supervision*), cut one 28 ½″-length for cross stick and one 32½″-length for top-bottom stick.

11. To split stick ends, hold exacto knife as shown (sharp edge of blade up) on magazine. Gently but firmly, press each end of each stick lengthwise onto sharp blade edge, making slits about ¼″ deep.

12. Place kite *right side down*, as shown. To attach sticks to kite, work first with cross stick (the shorter one). Fit left string loop into one split stick end, then fit on right loop (a). Next, fit top loop onto one end of longer stick. Then, pulling bottom loop taut, fit it into other end of this stick, which will bow up slightly. Press bowed stick down, covering line B (*step 2*), so bow is now pushing toward front of kite. Cut short length of string and tie cross sticks together in center (b). *Note:* If any stick ends should break at the split, repair with masking tape.

13. To prevent stick splits from widening, cut four pieces of string about 8″ long and tie one tightly around split end of each stick just *inside* point where loop rests, as shown.

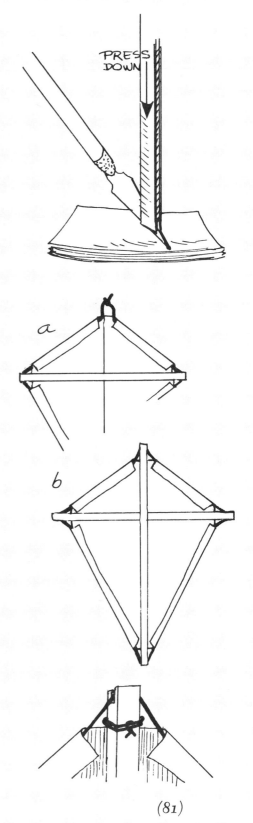

14. Cut a piece of string 60" long to make a "bridle." Tie one end (with double knot) to end of top stick. Then measure and mark string at point 31" down from knot. Pull string taut, making kite bow out slightly, and tie at 31" mark to end of bottom stick. This will leave about two feet of string hanging down below kite to form tail (*see step 15*). Flying line will later be attached to bridle.

15. To make tail, cut six rag or old sheet strips 1½" wide by 6" long. (You may wish to cut extra strips now so you will have them in case extra tail is needed when flying kite). At 4" intervals, tie tail string around center of cloth strips as shown. *Note:* It is the amount of tail surface, rather than its weight, which resists the wind and balances the kite. If your kite does not fly smoothly, try shortening or lengthening the tail. (Take extra string, rags, and scissors with you when flying kite.) At the same time, adjust placement of flying string (*see step 16*) on bridle, as it may need to be tied nearer to kite top or bottom.

16. In center of 12"-long, round stick, tie and knot, then wind on all remaining string, as shown. When flying kite, you will hold on to ends of stick (arrows) and string will unwind quickly and freely from center. Tie end of flying string about ⅓ of the way down from top of bridle (*step 14*). Kite is now ready to fly. Adjust tail length and flying string position to meet wind conditions and improve smoothness of flight (*see note, step 15*).

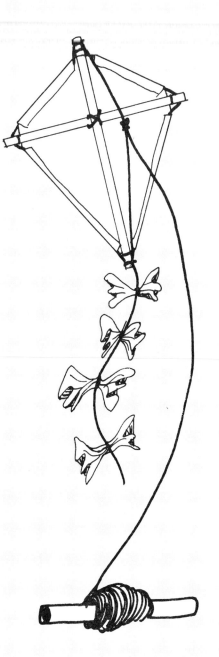

SHAVUOT

In ancient times, Jewish farmers brought an offering of barley, called an *omer*, to the Temple on the second day of Pesach. On this day, the counting of the weeks began, for according to Jewish law, on the fiftieth day after the bringing of the omer, the festival of *Shavuot* would be celebrated. For this reason, Shavuot is known as the "Festival of Weeks." It is observed on the sixth and seventh days of Sivan (May–June). The Greek word for *shavuot* (weeks) is *pentekoste,* and when the Old Testament was translated into Greek from Hebrew, the holiday became known among Greek-speaking Jews as Pentecost, and later served as the source for the Christian holy day of that name.

Just as Pesach was the time of the barley harvest, Shavuot was the festival of the wheat harvest. A sheaf of wheat and two loaves, called "wave loaves," made from the new flour, were offered to God as "first fruits" in a feast of thanksgiving. Thus, Shavuot is sometimes called the "Festival of First Fruits." Today in America and in Israel, Jewish homes and temples are decorated with fruits and flowers, and God is thanked for the harvest.

In Israel, Shavuot is usually celebrated in agricultural settlements and schools with special ceremonies honoring the first fruits. Decorative baskets of fruit are displayed. Children make decorations of fruit and flowers for their schools, homes, and temple. Boys and girls wear daisy or evergreen crowns in their hair.

As a religious holiday, Shavuot has another, perhaps more important meaning. According to tradition, it was on this day that God gave Moses the Ten Commandments on Mount Sinai. Moses led the Jews out of slavery in Egypt, and after six weeks, they arrived near Mount Sinai in the desert. God then spoke to Moses, telling him to gather his people beneath the mountain to receive the law of God. Three days later, after special purification rites, the people gathered at the base of the mountain. There God gave to Moses the two stone tablets on which were carved Ten Commandments, the basis of the Torah. In the synagogue on Shavuot today, there are ceremonies in honor of the giving of the Ten Commandments. The story of Ruth is read during the service, as she was an especially pious Jewess, and the great-grandmother of King David, who was born on Shavuot.

In the Middle Ages, it was the custom for children to begin their study of the Jewish religion on Shavuot. Today Reform and Conservative boys and girls are often confirmed on this day.

In memory of the agricultural significance of Shavuot, favorite holiday foods are *blintzes* (rolled or folded pancakes filled with cheese or fruit), fresh fruits, and milk and honey, which are eaten to recall the sweetness of the land and the sweetness of the Torah. Cakes and cookies, and even fruit arrangements are sometimes formed into mountain shapes to remind us of Mount Sinai.

 ## SHAVUOT FRUIT MOUNTAIN

One of these decorative fruit "mountains" may be made large enough for a buffet table centerpiece, or several small ones may be made for individual servings.

Materials: Fresh whole fruit (small bite-size fruit is best, such as grapes of various colors, strawberries, raspberries, cherries, dates, etc.), two large bunches of parsley or watercress, two boxes of colored toothpicks, styrofoam cone (at least 12″ to 14″ tall for large centerpiece), paring knife, serving platter, tinfoil.

1. Cover entire styrofoam cone with tinfoil, wrapped tightly around.

2. Arrange cone, point up, in center of platter. Wash fruit. Cut any large fruit, such as pineapple, into bite-size pieces. Set prepared fruit and toothpicks nearby. Beginning at the bottom of the cone and working upward to the tip, pierce each piece of fruit with a toothpick, then stick the pick into the cone. Work around in rings, placing the fruit as close together as possible without bruising the pieces. A striped effect may be had by making alternate rings of different colored fruits.

3. After the cone is covered with as much fruit as possible, top with a strawberry, cherry, or sprig of parsley or cress. Stick small sprigs of parsley or cress into any open spaces between fruit to hide the tinfoil. Hold sprigs in with toothpicks. Arrange a border of greens around base of cone. Chill in refrigerator until ready to serve.

SHAVUOT FLOWER FAVOR

This flower doubles as a place card and a favor for your Shavuot party table.

Materials: Colored construction paper, pencil, ruler, scissors, rubber cement, fluted paper muffin cups or small paper cups, crayons or felt pens.

1. Cut six colored paper petals—each leaf-shaped, about 4″ long, 1½″ wide at middle (a). Cut five between-petal shapes—each 4″ long with circle about ½″ across at one end (b). Cut one green stem ¾″ wide, 7″ long (c). Cut two green leaves—each about 3¾″ long, 1″ wide (d).

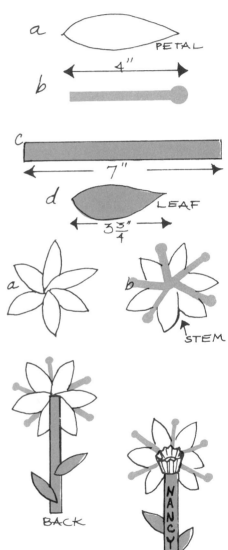

2. Arrange petals in a circle as shown (a), over-lapping and gluing the tips together. Then glue on the five between-petal designs (b). The stem will later be glued into the sixth space (*arrow*).

3. Turn flower over, face down. Glue end of stem to glued centers. Glue leaf tips onto stem.

4. Turn flower over, face up. Glue bottom of fluted muffin cup or small paper cup onto flower center.

5. Write guest's name down stem front with pen or crayon. Fill cup with small gifts or candies and set a flower favor beside each place at your Shavuot party table.

(85)

HOW TO TRACE AND TRANSFER PATTERNS

Always trace patterns, *never* cut book, or you will destroy the directions on the other side of the page, and will not have the patterns to reuse year after year.

1. Place a piece of tracing paper over the whole pattern you want to copy. Pull edges of tracing paper over book and tape them to table to hold drawing steady.

2. With pencil, lightly trace pattern outline onto tracing paper. (If you press too hard, you will tear through tracing and into book.) Also trace dotted lines, which mean *fold,* and all other markings *within* pattern.

3. Lift tracing off book and place it *face down* on scrap paper. With soft, dark pencil, rub all over *back* of tracing (a). To transfer onto dark colored paper, rub with white chalk instead of pencil. *Note:* Instead of scribbling on back of tracing, you can place a sheet of carbon paper, *black side down,* between tracing and paper, and draw over it to transfer pattern (b).

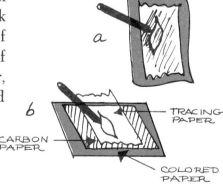

4. Compare transferred pattern to original in book to be sure that you have traced all lines. Pattern is now ready to be cut out.

HOW TO SCORE PAPER

To make a neat fold in a stiff piece of paper, the surface of the paper may be scored, or lightly cut, with a sharp knife. Scoring is not necessary for soft papers which fold easily. *Note:* SCORING IS DONE WITH A SHARP KNIFE, OR EXACTO KNIFE, AND THEREFORE CAN BE DANGEROUS. DO NOT USE KNIFE WITHOUT PERMISSION OR ADULT SUPERVISION.

To Score a Line:

1. Before scoring, decide in which direction you will want fold to close. The scored edge should be on the *outside*. Place paper on table *outside surface up.*

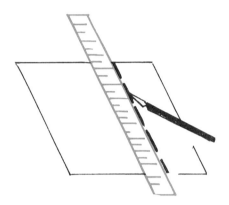

2. Hold ruler against dotted "fold" line to be scored. Run knife along ruler's edge very lightly, with one stroke, cutting only surface of paper, slightly deeper than a scratch. DO NOT CUT THROUGH PAPER.

3. Now fold paper along scored line, keeping cut surface on *outside* of fold. Press fold flat.

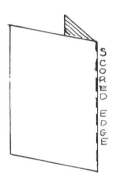

SCORED EDGE

MATERIALS

The following is a list of all the materials mentioned in this book although each project will require the use of only a few at a time. Materials can easily be found in your home, local stationery store, 5 & 10 cent store, art supply or craft shop, hardware or grocery store. If you have any trouble, look in the yellow pages of the phone book. Use the materials suggested or make up your own variations.

Note: Throughout this book, the symbol ′ has been used for *feet* and ″ for *inches.* Before beginning any project, read all the directions through to the end. Read the instructions on tracing and transferring patterns.

ruler, yardstick
pencil, colored pencils, crayons
pen, colored felt or nylon-tipped pens
scissors (regular shears), small manicure scissors
stapler
exacto knife, small paring knife
paper clips
masking and cellophane tape, florists' tape (green tape found in a flower shop
    or stationery store)
rubber cement, white glue
paper towels
newspapers
wax paper
thread
wool (varying thicknesses, bright colors)
embroidery thread or yarn, raffia
string (medium thick, white cotton)
wire (#32 thread wire on spool, cotton covered optional), "stem wire" (made
    for paper flowers, usually comes wrapped in green thread; use medium
    heavy weight that is strong yet fairly flexible, in 27″ lengths)
wire cutters
pliers
styrofoam cone (12″–14″ tall)

candles (standard wax table candles about ¾" in diameter, Hanukah candles found in packages in stationery or food stores)

embroidery needles, fine sewing needles

fluted paper muffin cups or small paper cups

toothpicks, colored

orange stick (for manicuring nails, to be used as clay modeling tool)

clean empty tin cans (one end removed)

wooden dowel or stick (about ¼" in diameter)

balsa wood (found in hobby shops and hardware stores)

tinfoil, colored foil

crepe paper (double-weight or duplex and single-weight)

construction paper, decorative gift wrapping paper, colored tissue paper, tracing paper

assorted decorative trimmings (gold braid, ribbon, feathers, old costume jewelry, lace, beads, etc.)

cardboard, shirt cardboard, bristol board (2-ply), heavy mat board or corrugated cardboard.

cardboard tube (from paper towel or wax paper roll or gift wrapping paper roll)

cardboard box (stationery or note-paper box at least 3¾" by 4¾" by 3")

tempera paint or water colors (water base and washable)

paint brush

white shellac and shellac brush

denatured alcohol (solvent for washing shellac brush)

chalk

plasticene clay

self-hardening clay (found in art supply stores, does not require firing in a kiln; label will indicate whether or not clay may be used with a wire armature)

plaster of paris (found in art supply or hardware store)

clear krylon and colored enamel spray (found in art supply or hardware store)

cookie sheet or marble slab

apple corer

mixing bowl

wooden spoon

spatula

measuring spoons and cups

emery board or sandpaper

non-evergreen tree branch

FOODS
almonds (blanched, whole and slivered)
baking powder, baking soda
butter (or margarine)
cooking oil
eggs, white
flour
fruit, whole fresh (strawberries, cherries, dates, lemons, figs, grapes, etc.)
ginger, powdered
honey
parsley or watercress
poppy seeds
prunes (12-ounce can of prune "butter" or pastry filling or cooked pitted prunes put through food mill)
salt
sugar
walnuts, shelled

INDEX